HEALING POWER OF AURA & SOUL PORTRAITS

Una Jasmin White Ph.D.
Artistic Medium, Healer & Art Color Light Therapist

"The publication of this book is dedicated to the memory of Una Jasmin White, and released in time for her memorial in June, 2018. Una's passion and mission was to publish her Great Work. Originally in two parts, I have combined them both, keeping the content as Una wrote it, only editing and formatting where necessary. It is a great honor to have been charged with the editing of Una's work for publishing. A legacy from Una, to humanity as a whole."

In Divine Love and gratitude,
Karen Tants,
on behalf of © Sundi and Joseph Sturgeon
Angelic Light Book Distribution
Holistic Light Rejuvenation Center
A 501c3 Charitable Organisation
www.holisticrejuvenate.com

All Rights Reserved
No part of this publication may be reproduced, stored in a retrieval system, or transmitted in any form or by any means, electrical, mechanical, photocopying, recording or otherwise, without the prior written consent of the publisher.

IRMGARD HELLICH (UNA JASMIN) WHITE – 1946 - 2017
Introduction to my first e-book

About twenty years ago my celestial husband encouraged me to create a book to share my work as a soul portrait artist with the world. Twenty years later I am feeling that it's time to keep my promise and commitment to fulfil our legacy. The everlasting loving presence of my beloved twin flame, John, connected with me, works with me from the world of light, inspiring me to continue our legacy to 'unite heaven and earth', revealing and communicating limitless Divine Love and Light shining through my soul portraits and healing art with life-transforming messages from this and the Other Side.

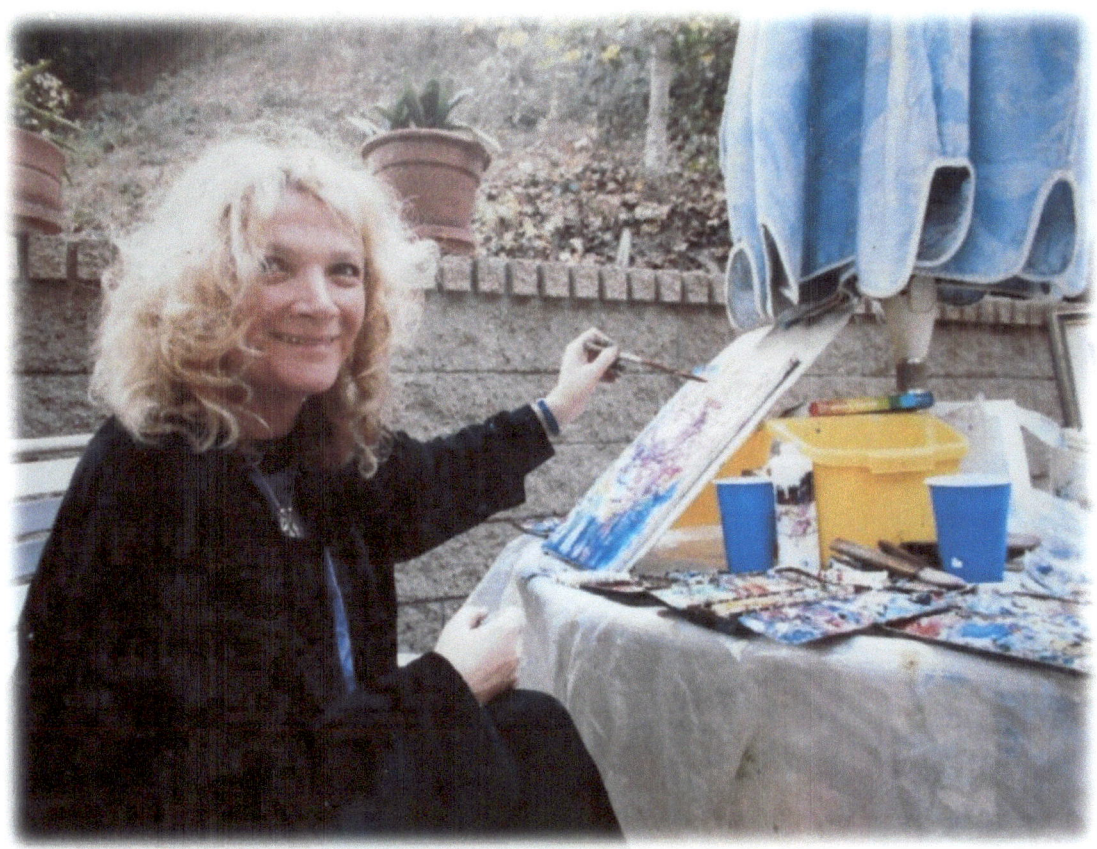

I am feeling blessed to co-create God's work through my luminous art, changing the world one-soul-at-a-time, making the magical experience of the Divine, a loving reality.

This first book is offering a glance into my pioneering work as a visionary soul portrait artist, present in collections worldwide. It is inviting you on a journey into different Soul-scapes (portraits) revealing the unique light and beauty of each soul; as expression of the Divine-Human nature of each person, pet, departed loved one, and inspirational personalities from the world of light, with specific messages that may touch your heart and inspire your spirit.

May this book awaken your desire to:

Access, ignite the fire of your soul and your highest soul potential, awaken and express your unique Divine-Human being-ness, special Divine qualities (spiritual gifts), Divine life's purpose and your tools for transformation, fulfilment and wholeness through a shift of consciousness on the path toward enlightenment.

The visual experience of one's soul journey via the transformational color/light vibrations with channelled messages from this and the Other Side, the resonance with the soul portrait is a continuous healing opportunity, aligning you with your highest soul's frequency, connecting you with your guides, angels, and departed loved ones. It's an opportunity to experience the aliveness, infinite love, light and wisdom emanating from your soul. Living in resonance with your heart and soul; your soul's love and wisdom, aligned with your soul's purpose, empowers your life and the lives of loved ones. You will feel protected, strong, and inspired to make Divinely guided decisions.

"Remembering who you really are as a Divine-Human being, and why you are here at this time, you will fall in love with your True Self."

You may be inspired by some stories of people living in this reality, by departed loved ones, or by an inspirational leader; (Yogananda or Beethoven shining their light into your soul) because their special qualities, energies and messages may 'strike a chord within you', uplift you, or awaken qualities or insights you need right now in your life.

Mission Statement

It is my passion to reveal the loving interconnectedness of 'all-that-is' between heaven and earth. The energy of Divine Light and Love connecting us all, is boundless and life goes on. This book may be an inspiration to connect with departed loved ones or anyone important to you.

My channelled healing soul portraits promote personal, spiritual and planetary transformation. These luminous soul portraits empower us to transmute any negativity, obstacles or limitations that hinder us from becoming our true Divine Selves, which is simply LOVE.

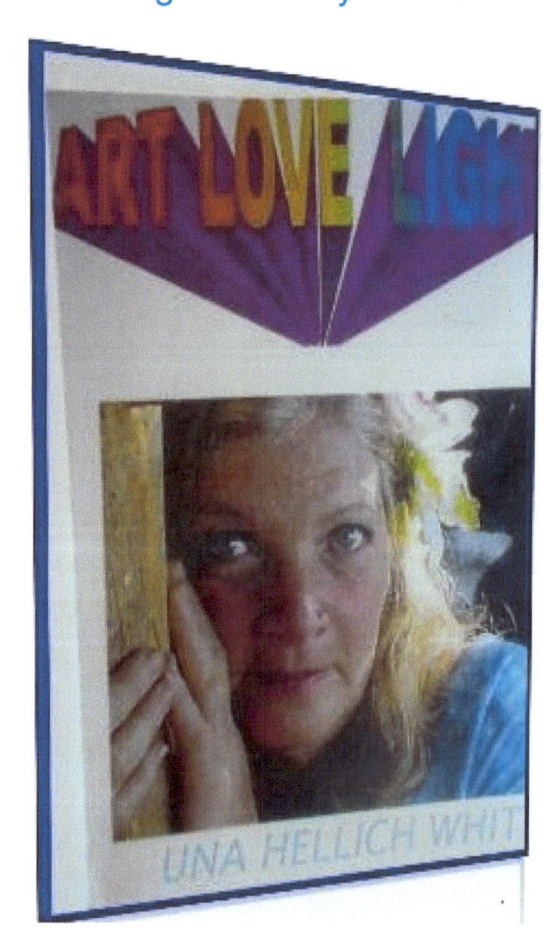

May this book inspire, delight, uplift and educate you, promote true compassion, wholeness, joy and peace; create the awareness that the Divine Love and Light is within all of us, waiting to be expressed and shared; inspire us to change the world one-soul-at-a-time; create the desire to become part of a conscious evolution toward a new Divinely inspired humanity-society.

In the second part of this book, I reveal the dynamic interplay between couples, compatibility, complementarity, soul mates, twin flames, more departed loved ones, famous personalities such as Angela Merkel. I had the opportunity to paint Arnold Schwartzenegger's soul portrait in Austria, in the garden of his museum.

Purpose

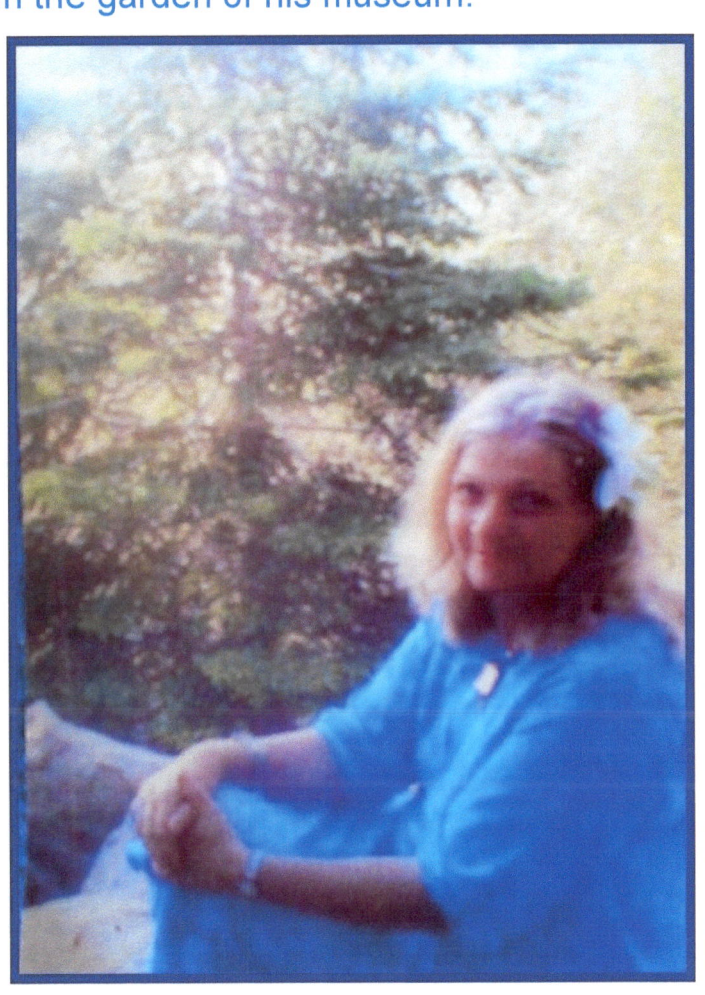

It is my purpose to inspire people to discover themselves as Divine beings, to experience the loving presence and aliveness, guidance and power of their soul, to actualize their highest potential guiding them to true fulfilment, peace, harmony in relationships, and to experience the joy of wholeness.

I am happy to assist people to move through life's challenges, to adapt to life's changes with grace and ease, and to work in synchronicity with the universe, aligned with the highest energies of light.

My Plan for the future

A **Coffee Table Book**, spanning my experience as an artistic master medium, healer, and transpersonal art therapist; offering tools of transpersonal art therapy including working with auras, energies, color, love and light. My plan is to create soul portraits of important world leaders inspiring them to act and impact their lives and the lives of others from the love and wisdom of their soul; such as **Angela Merkel**. I have created the soul portraits of **Senator and Governor of Hawaii Akaka**, and **Arnold Schwartzenegger** in the garden of his museum in Thal Bei Graz, Austria.

"It will happen. The future is now!"

Dedication

My infinite gratitude to my family, my beloved parents, my daughter with her family, my beloved husband John White; who's everlasting loving presence continues to support and inspire me from the world of light, and who encouraged me to create our book twenty years ago.

I thank my Sufi teacher, Pir Vilayat Inayat Khan, for his life-changing teachings. Pir initiated me into my name, Una; meaning art in Sanskrit, which has inspired me to create Healing Soul Portraits. I am grateful to Guy Coggins, the inventor of the aura camera for introducing, promoting and sponsoring my work in the United States since 1991. I am immensely grateful for the continuous support, healing and inspiration of my dear friends in Europe (Austria and France), in Hawaii, Long Island and California. I thank Da Vid, the Light Party, for his continuous loving inspiration and support. My gratitude to my dear friend **Scott 'Sky' Masters**, for his amazing collaboration creating this book.

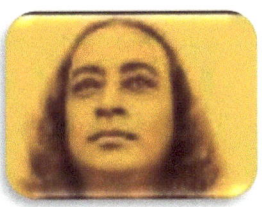

Paramahansa Yogananda

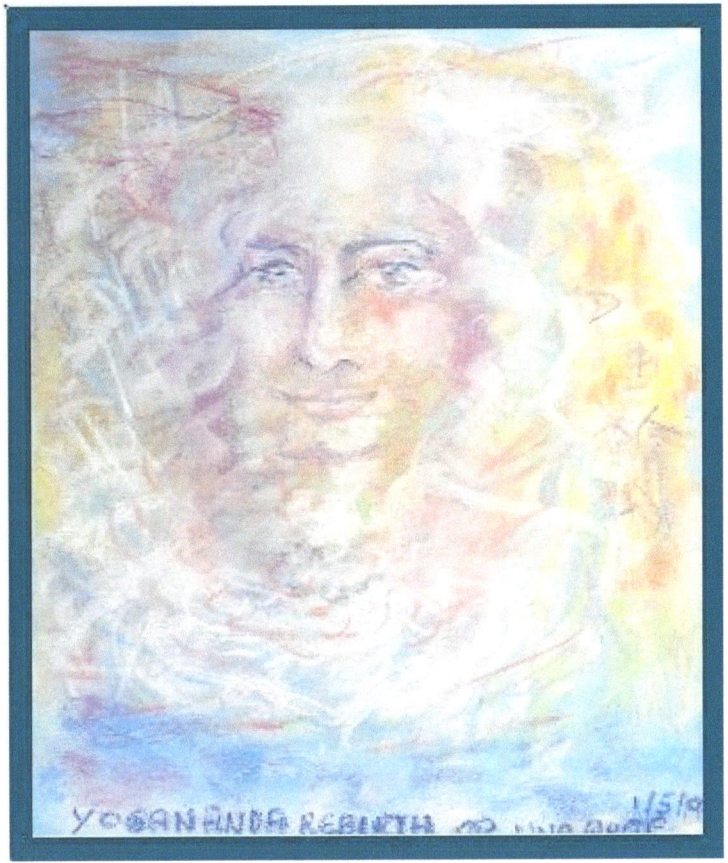

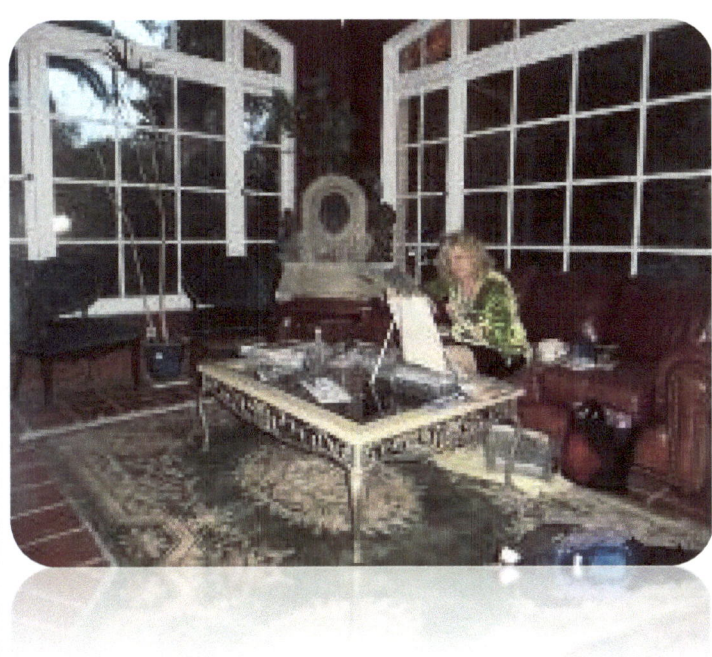

The new human DNA

is DIVINE LOVE

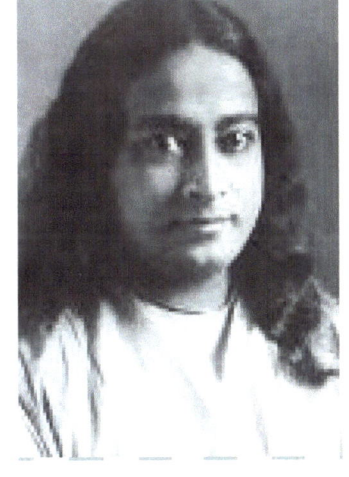

I created this soul portrait at Ortega's mansion; dedicated to Paramahansa Yogananda on the anniversary of his birthday: January 5th, 2013, San Diego, Ca.

I thank the spirit of Yogananda, who's work I discovered in a second hand bookshop in San Francisco many years ago. His Self-Realization agendas have been of great support, guidance and inspiration ever since.

"The deeper the self-realization of man, the more he influences the whole universe by his subtle spiritual vibrations."

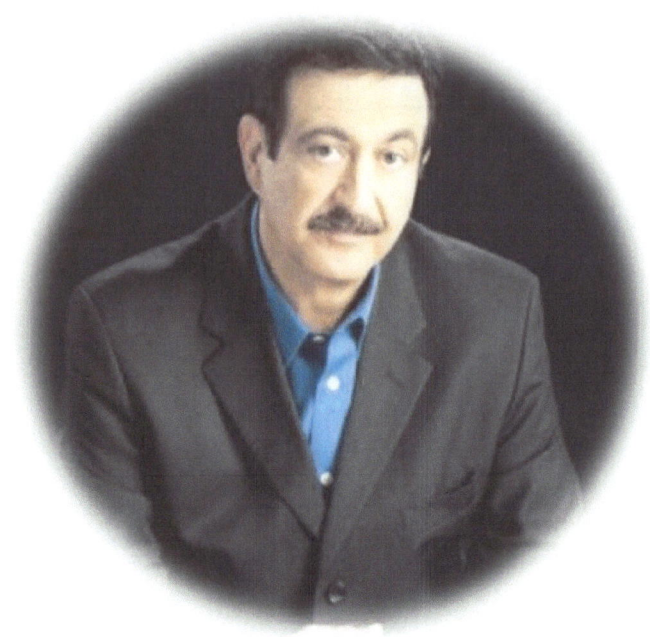

George Noory soul portrait and streamed information created by Una White on the Big Island in 2011.

I have listened to Coast to Coast A.M. for many years and appreciated George via his radio shows and meetings during various events in person. In 2012 I had the pleasure to offer him his soul portrait painted on the Big Island in 2011, which he loves very much. Number one talk show host of Coast to Coast A.M. and of his own TV show (predicted by me).

George is a bright star illuminating the lives of up to ten million listeners worldwide. He is gifted with a compassionate, extraordinary skill of interviewing; attracting the most famous guests from a wide variety of disciplines (spirituality, medicine, paranormal, economics) sharing their pioneering knowledge; Shirley Maclaine, James Van Praagh, Dannion Brinkley, Bruce Goldberg, Deepak Chopra, David Wilcock among many others.

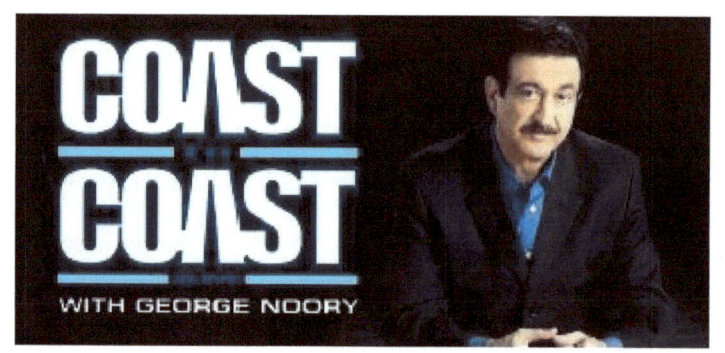

His soul colors: Purple, Gold, White, Yellow, Orange, Greens and Blues.

Deeply spiritual, George has a brilliant, innovative, visionary spirit of great wisdom, sensibility, creativity, intuition and an intimate connectedness with the universe. George is able to see the truth from a Divine perspective, with eyes capable to see different realities, with an acute perception of the continuum of all realities simultaneously.

Creating a quantum field of new possibilities, dimensions, realities, he prepares people for the change, for challenging times and coming events ahead by promoting a paradigm shift for justice, freedom, and wholeness for all. Raising consciousness, offering hope, his service to the planet has the potential to transform suffering and ignorance into healing, knowledge, serenity and peace.

George has the courage and strength to overcome any struggles, as he is very loved, supported and protected by many beings of light, archangels, masters, powerful guides and guardians, assisting him to realize his heart's desire, and to promote his visions of planetary liberation.

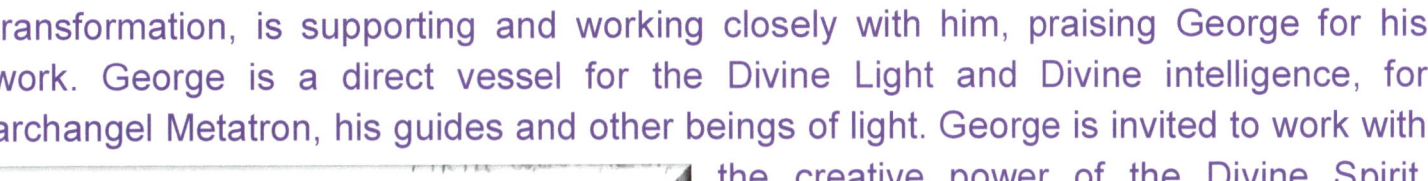

St. Germain, an ascended master; the alchemist, streaming **purple** rays of transmutation and transformation, is supporting and working closely with him, praising George for his work. George is a direct vessel for the Divine Light and Divine intelligence, for archangel Metatron, his guides and other beings of light. George is invited to work with the creative power of the Divine Spirit, speaking through him to inspire others THROUGH him, to co-create the new paradigm.

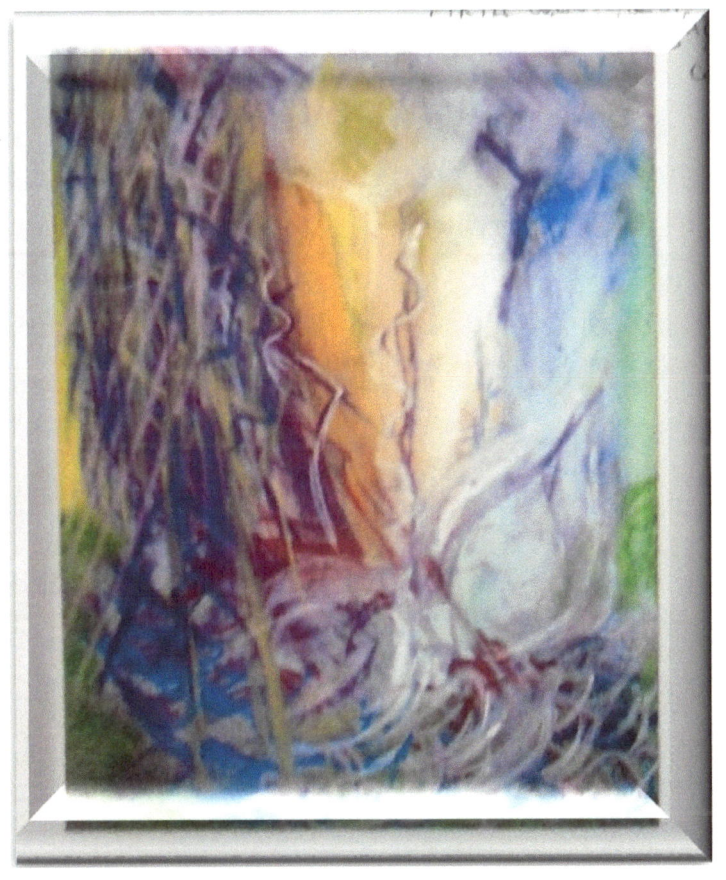

George's soul, his Divine DNA, in **white** and **purple,** representing his mystical, spiritual Divine Self, is emerging from the purple realm, from a magnificent temple of amethysts; a configuration of sacred geometry. This sanctuary is filled with brilliant **white**, **golden**, **orange light**. George is gifted to work with and bring forth the energies of golden, white and orange rays of wisdom, creativity and healing. George has spent many lives in temples or sacred spaces.

The **white** sphere above George's head (see his forehead), represents his direct connection, close relationship, and one-ness with Divine presence, the Divine Light, and with archangel Metatron (major inspiration). His one-ness with Divine is offering George a deep understanding of unity and the interconnectedness of all that is connected through the Divine Light.

It's a good time for George to develop his creativity (**orange**), leading him into yet unexplored territory.

Green; a virgin green, representing the new earth, harmony, love of nature, growth, renewal and healing.

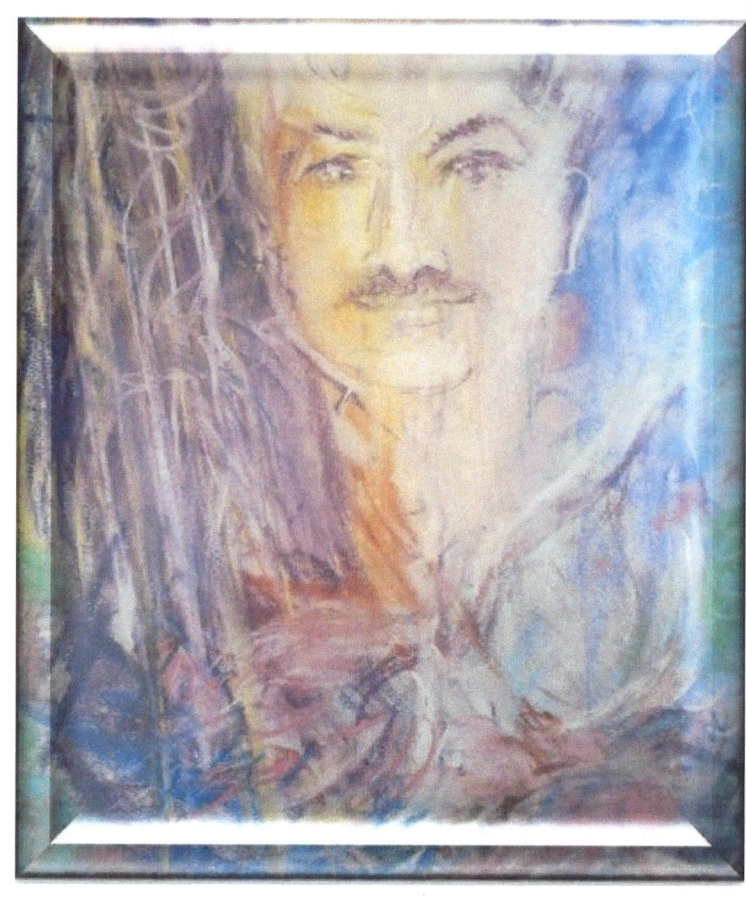

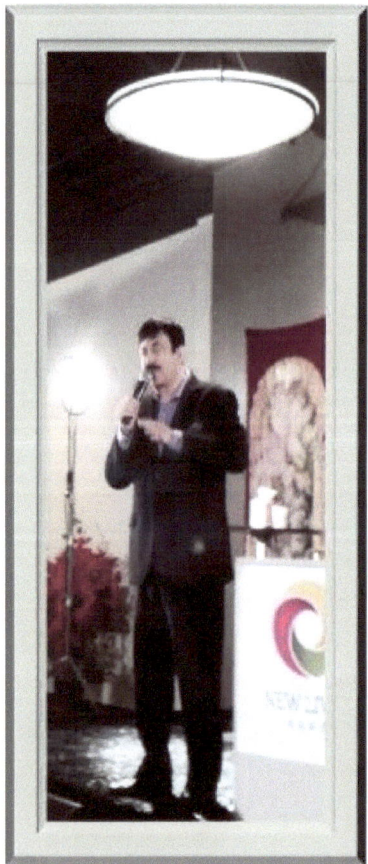

Blue on the right; dreams, traveling into other dimensions, time travel, connections with beings from other dimensions. A guide is inspiring and supporting him to manifest his visions and dreams; to create and manifest a new vision for humanity. Secrets for transforming a dense, dark reality into a more subtle reality filled with clarity, truth,
light and love are being revealed to him.

George is in a period of his life achieving ever-growing success, with love surrounding him and with miracles on his way. George's colourful life path propels him toward enlightenment; it's a way of love, love is the goal, opening pathways to higher dimensions and enlightenment for others. Enjoy the colourful rainbows of life; just take the time to relax, there is a possibility to purchase a property in Hawaii in the future.

Believe in the power of your eyes, in the power of your vision, your gift to see through the veil of illusion, because everything in the universe is transparent to you, offering you deep insights from all times. You have the magnetic power to awaken, open and move the hearts and minds of many, guiding humanity toward Divinely guided fulfilment. Wholeness and enlightenment.

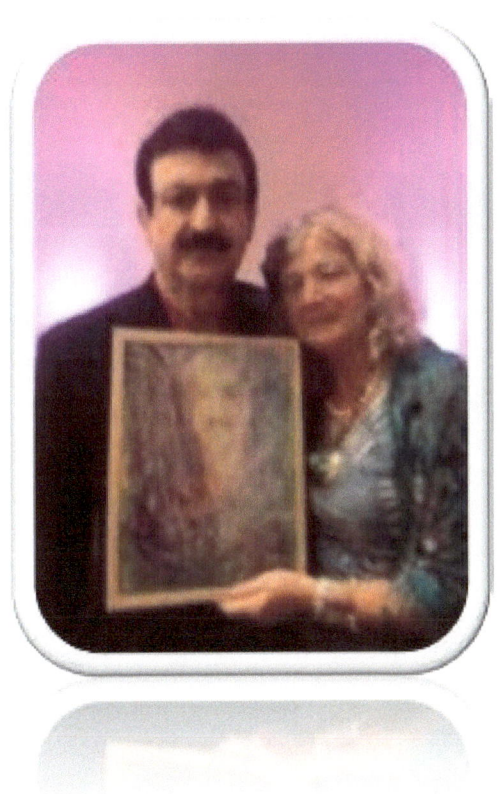

Liliuokalani, the last Queen of Hawaii
Painted on Makapu'u Beach, Oahu, Hawaii

Shining her light and mysterious beauty from beyond, Liliuokalani wants to be remembered for her artistic, intuitive talents. She continues the legacy of her endearing spirit for all the children of Hawaii from the Other Side. I was drawn to paint her soul portrait from the Other Side on Makapu'u beach, Oahu. I understood later, why I felt her vibrational presence so strongly in this place: It used to be her summer residence.

Liliuokalani had a very happy, joyful nature. It was her passion and commitment to keep the spirit of Aloha alive and to preserve the freedom of the people of Hawaii. Affirming the importance of **Liberty for Hawaii**; she says that the sacredness of the Hawaiian traditions and its culture will always prevail, no matter what.

Very devoted to the people of her kingdom, especially to the well-being, education and happiness of the children, and to women's empowerment, she reminds the people of Hawaii: **"Do not give up, never lose confidence, courage, self-acceptance and joy."**

Liliuokalani created schools, she was a mother to all; protective and compassionate, majestic and powerful.

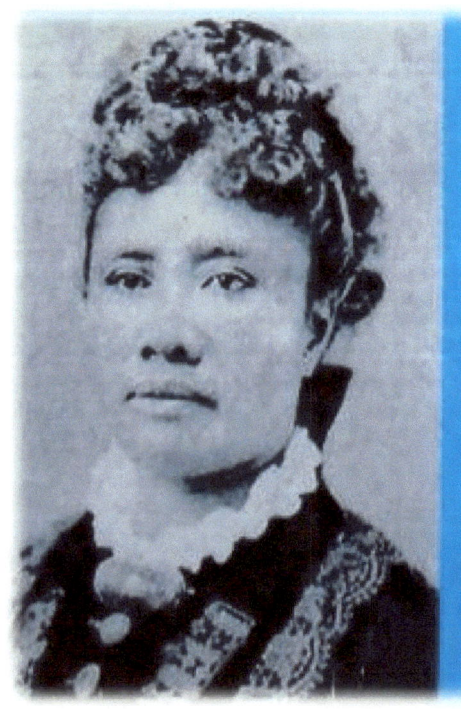

This soul portrait is to reconstitute and reveal her power as a Queen; honouring her spiritual and terrestrial power, intact, always very connected to the spirit world and the terrestrial world at the same time. Emerging from the ocean as a beautiful flower of Hawaii, she is shining that light, from her crown of flowers of light, representing the beauty of Hawaii, long beyond her mortality. The white flowers symbolize her innocence. She wants to be perceived and remembered as innocent, for her beauty, artistic and intuitive talents, passions, and for all she did for the children of Hawaii and in the world. She feels, and always will feel, like a devoted mother for many.

It's a good time for new energies to come, and to pray, act and believe in miracles.

Soul colors: Purple, Gold, Yellow, White, Colors of the Oceans.

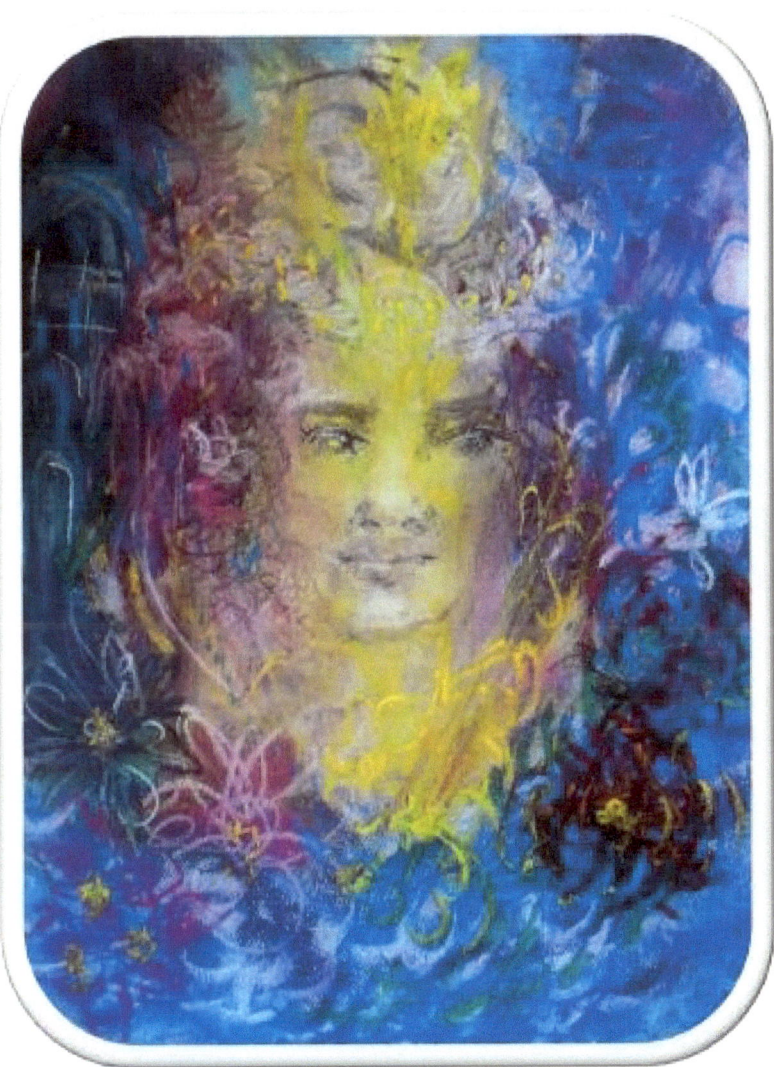

Liliuokalani loved purple, gold and yellow as well as the colors of the oceans.

Purple represents her spiritual gifts. She prayed a lot; her intimate connection with God kept her strong. She enjoyed solitude. She enjoyed to dream; her music and poetry were her prayer; her inner bridge to God. Her spiritual approach to life was rooted in past lives, where she had a sacred function as a High Priestess. Fascinated by the mysteries of the universe and the Divine, she believed in Divine magic and encourages us to believe in Divine magic and miracles also.

On the right: A magical wand, representing gifts of magic and manifestation. Liliuokalani feels that these energies can be re-activated and communicated to those who are ready to connect with her and to receive her messages from beyond, revealing empowering teaching tools, to create more happiness, strength, confidence, wholeness, and miracles for the people of Hawaii.

Green: Love of nature, of flowers. She saw people as beautiful flowers; blooming. She enjoyed connecting and talking with nature spirits, fairies, and her ancestors, her friends and inspiration. Her favoured places were the Lao Valley on Maui and Makapu'u beach. She was very connected with the Kahuna's. She never gave up her inner power.

Blues and Greens; the Ocean: Her soul portrait is revealing the palace she is residing in on the Other Side.

Red: Loved red, she was very passionate; red is the color of creativity, love and life.

White on the forehead: Portal to God; a sacred writing appears, inspiration as she is accessing the Divine flowing through her sacred poetry and music. She is wearing a **crown of white flowers**, symbolizing her love of the sacredness of being, innocence and integrity. Even though she does not really like crowns, she does love crowns made from flowers; especially yellow, offering gifts of joy and happiness through the yellow flowers.

Gold: Gold in her eyes, expressing bliss and Divine happiness, felicity and Divine joy, shining onto us from beyond, enlightening our hearts. She has the eyes of an Owl; looking at life through eyes of wisdom, gifted with seeing the truth. The golden flower in the center represents her golden heart. It also represents the flower of life and is associated with the royal family. She still feels like a queen in the heavenly realms of light, radiating the nobility of body/mind/spirit, and the triumphant Spirit of the Divine within, that can never be broken, no matter what.

It was Liliuokalani's deepest heart desire to save the children, offering children the opportunity to grow and bloom like flowers, to be cared for with love. Also offering them the opportunity to express their soul's needs, innocence, talents, aspirations and to be inspired by beauty, nature, to experience and create harmony, compassion for themselves and others.

May the memory of Liliuokalani's life and work inspire new ways of teaching, being and relating with each other. May inspiration, beauty, the love of nature, compassion, communication from the heart, peace and a revival of traditions become new corner stones for the new generations to come; **To enjoy the healing power of happiness and beauty....**

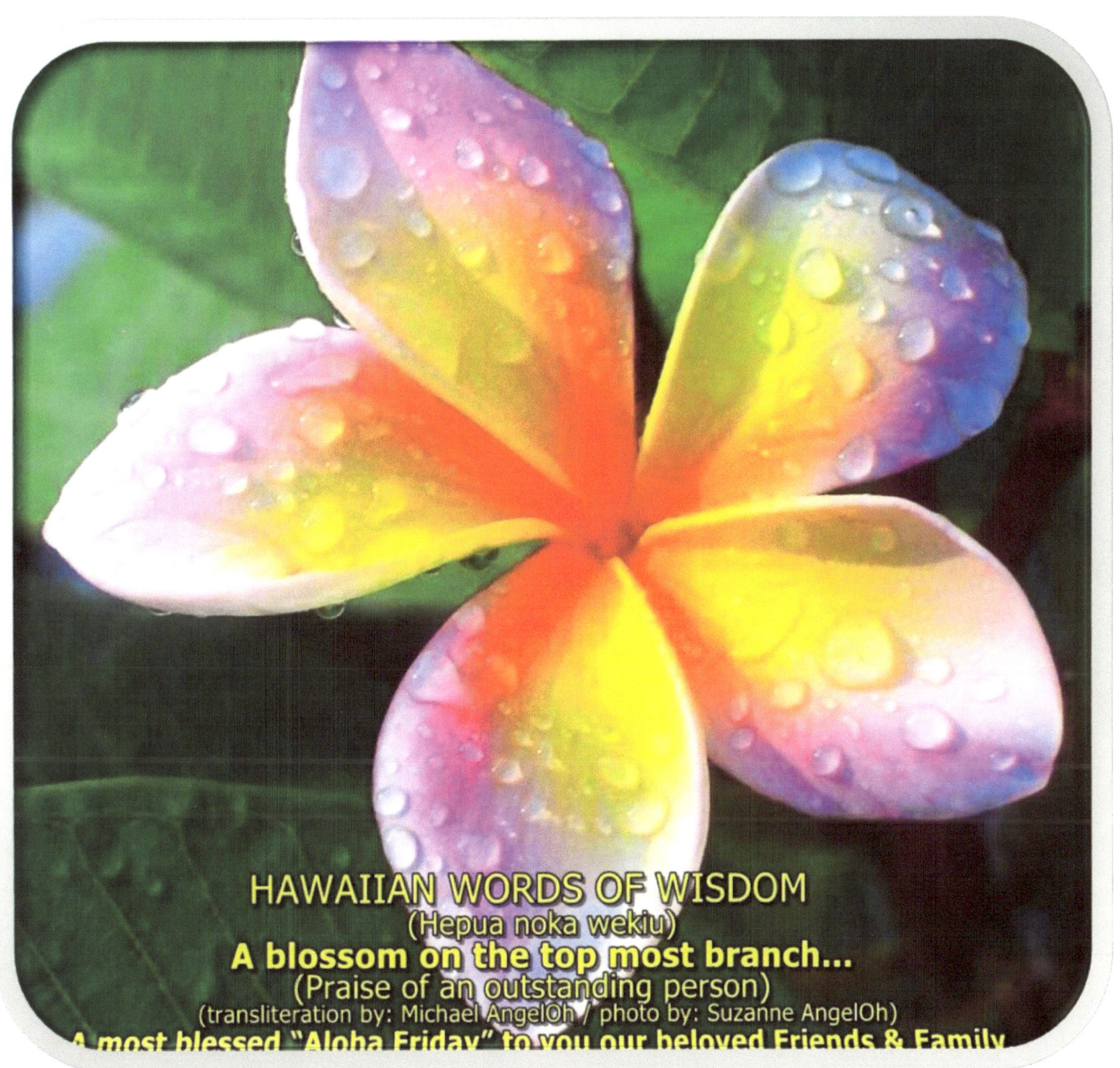

BROTHER IZ SOUL PORTRAIT PAINTED ON MAUI IN 2006

Almost twenty years ago I was guided to paint the soul portrait of Brother IZ. His music and messages, a call for peace and love, deeply touched my celestial husband's and my heart. I felt a natural connection with his personality and music because he embodied the spirit of aloha. I was honoured to meet his family and paint their soul portraits in Honolulu and to offer a copy of the soul portrait to his wife. He sees his wife as the spokeswoman for spreading the living power and message of aloha, to be proclaimed all over the world. He trusts that things come together. His music is also a tool; teaching truth, peace, happiness and success.

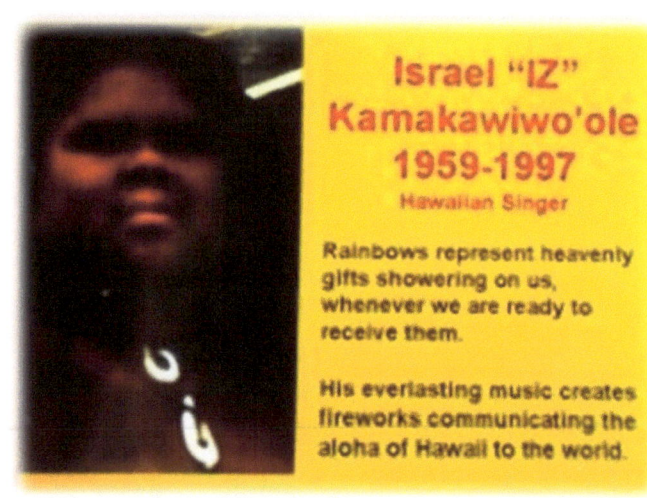

Brother IZ had amazing magical, healing, spiritual creative powers. He was fully aware of his role as a creative leader. He is working closely with us from the Other Side. He will not stop sending inspirations and guidance until his work is done. His legacy continues to spread the aloha spirit through his music around the globe. He feels that nothing is too difficult, listen to spirit and just do it. IZ loved the wind, listening to the messages coming from the wind. His soul portrait reveals a very strong personality, with great determination, who never gives up, encouraging us to do the same. Some people do not know any more what the true spirit of aloha is; there still will be a lot of struggle to re-establish the spirit and way of life of aloha, but there is hope for things to turn around for the best.

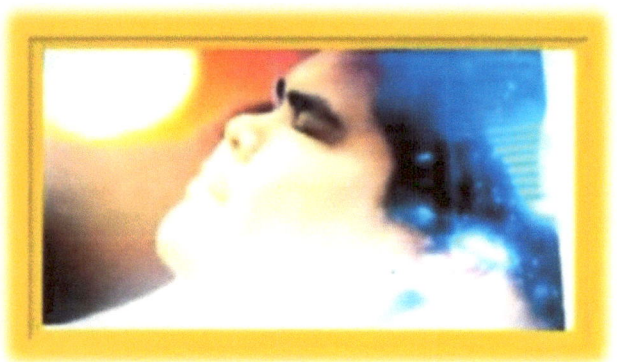

Soul colors: All the colors in the soul portrait represent the energies of Hawaii and also the energies of past kings. Brother IZ was connected with the Hawaiian kings; he had a certain royal way of being.

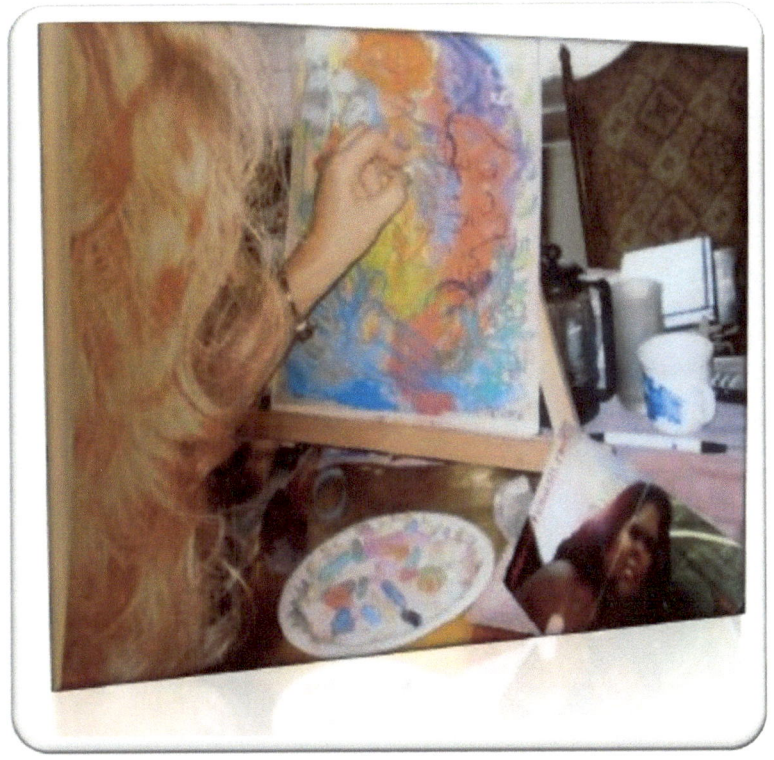

Many intense colors create the tapestry of his soul and how his soul is impregnated by the Hawaiian spirit: **Purples, Reds, Oranges, Yellows and Green;** his soul and spirit embody the aloha spirit, the creative spirit of the earth, the people, and the ancestors of Hawaii.

Purple: IZ had mystical spiritual and magical powers.

Red: Wings of fire, passion, original fire of creativity, his immense magical creative gifts flowing into him at all times. Red represents also Pele, the fire Goddess; a great inspiration, Pele is like a sister for Brother IZ.

Red and **Orange** together represent the creative power of life, his deep connection with the Sun as source of life. He loved sunrise and sunset. Brother IZ loved all the flowers, especially red and white flowers. He used to offer red flowers to his lovely wife, and is offering a red flower to her right now via this soul portrait (She confirmed that he offered her a special red flower as a declaration of his love). Many hearts, especially in orange, are communicating the love, life and creative energies coming from the Sun.

IZ, is ONE, with all the elements; the powers of nature. Loves the wind; spirit talks to him through the wind, lightning and thunder.

Green: Deep connection and love of nature; feeling part of nature, he is experiencing its presence and aliveness, supported by all the nature spirits. He is in love with the jungle, represented by the deep green color. He believes and has the vision that the earth of Hawaii will be renewed and healed. His throat is green, radiating harmony, the desire to co-create a new earth. He feels he is an open channel, experiencing the breath of spirit flowing through him when he is singing, communicating inspiration and harmonics from the heavens.

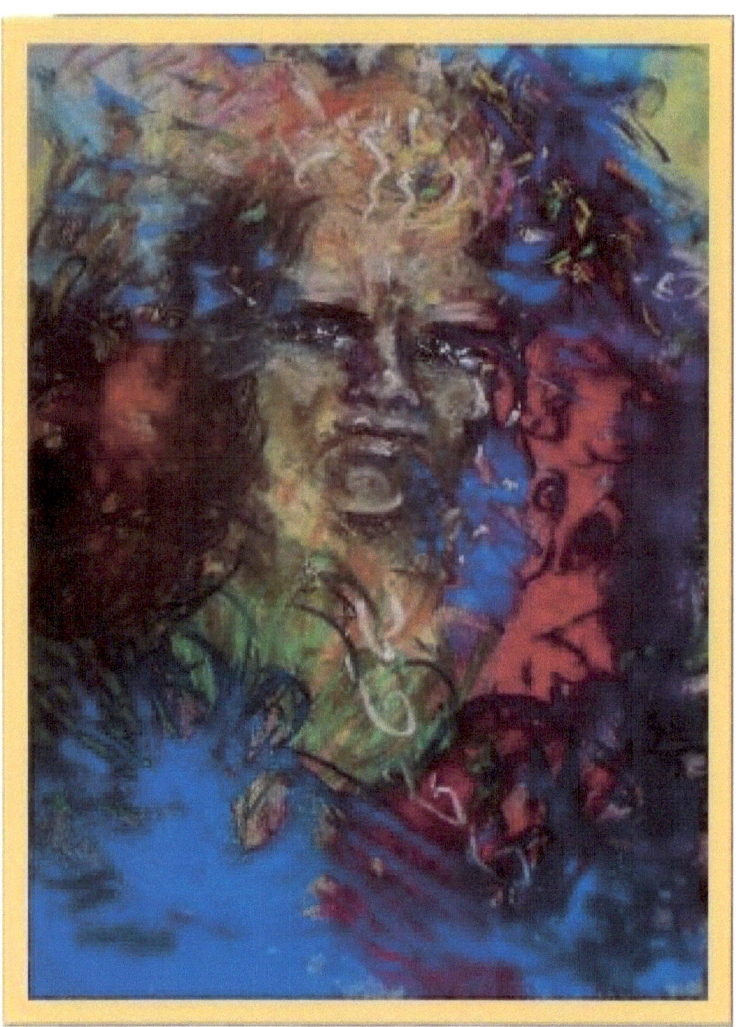

Blue: Represents loyalty, his desire for spreading peace, tenderness. A blue butterfly from heavenly dimensions brings him inspiration: Butterflies represent beings from other dimensions or the Other Side inspiring his songs with love and beauty. He loved butterflies.

Purple and **White** in his eyes: Communicating the creative magical power of spirit, and the victory of the spirit of aloha. The vital energy of spirit coming from the Sun is flowing through his crown chakra and third eye, sparkling rainbows and musical fireworks, ready to be shared with the world.

Brother IZ Message to Us

"The rainbow is not just a rainbow; its heavenly colors represent heavenly gifts showered on us. Every time we are ready to receive them like a sparkling firework, that is energy of ecstasy, bliss and peace. The sacredness of the rainbow is very important; it symbolizes transformation, hope, love, freedom and no more fear. The expression of our creative spirit in all life situations is essential for the survival of humanity. Believe in the victory of a restored Hawaii, have faith that victory, power of love and truth will prevail. Hawaiians, be aware of your brother and sisterhood, we are all working together in unity.

It is important to work together with Native Americans and all the other indigenous peoples. Don't give up your land, you are not alone, you have all our support from the spirit world. Set your intentions and transformation will come."

Brother IZ continues his leadership in the spirit world sending messages, inspirations and gifts of creativity. His legacy will prevail, and be spread all over the world, keeping the spirit of aloha alive; as a way of being and relating, as a way to live in harmony and respect for Mother Earth.

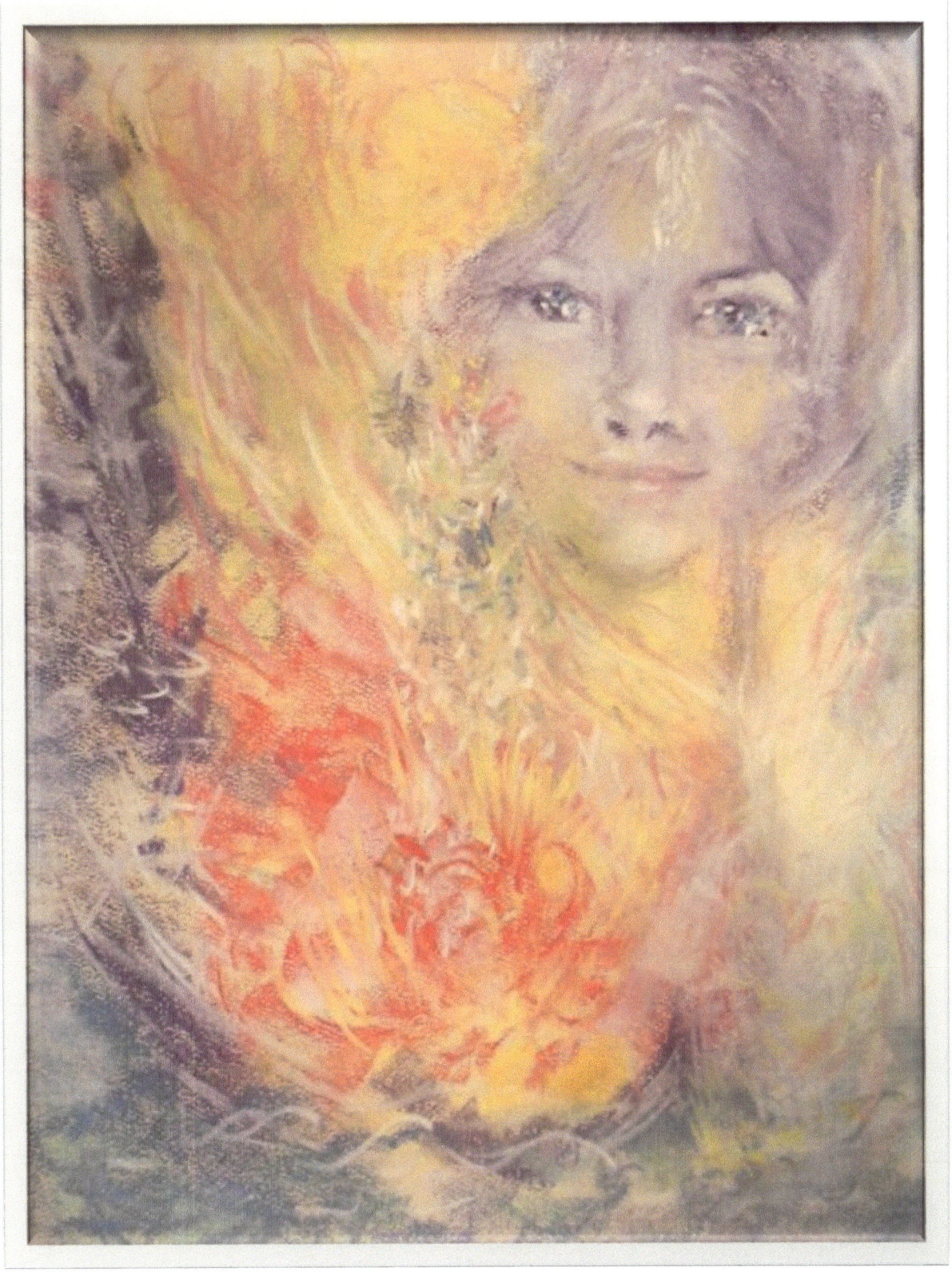

Truly an angel, with a sacred heart (embedded in her DNA), Mary radiates the presence of Divine Light, bringing gifts of felicity, joy, creativity, healing, hope and miracles.

ERIC BORDEAUX
PRINCE OF PEACE

Painted in 2000 in Southern California, on a sacred site, this painting represents the spiritual essence of Eric, revealing his mission as angelic messenger of PEACE, Divine Light and healing.

Eric, Angel of Peace and Healing

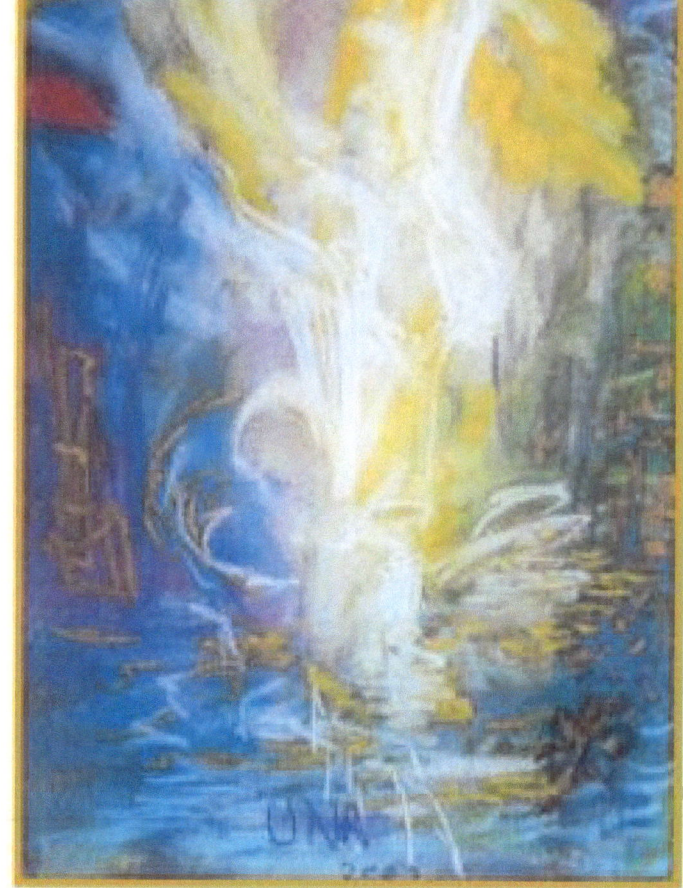

The soul portrait I painted of Eric, eleven years later confirmed his soul's purpose; his Divine mission: To offer his sacred gifts of infinite peace, bliss, Divinely inspired information, healings and enlightenment to the world. This soul portrait of Eric, living in Bordeaux, was created

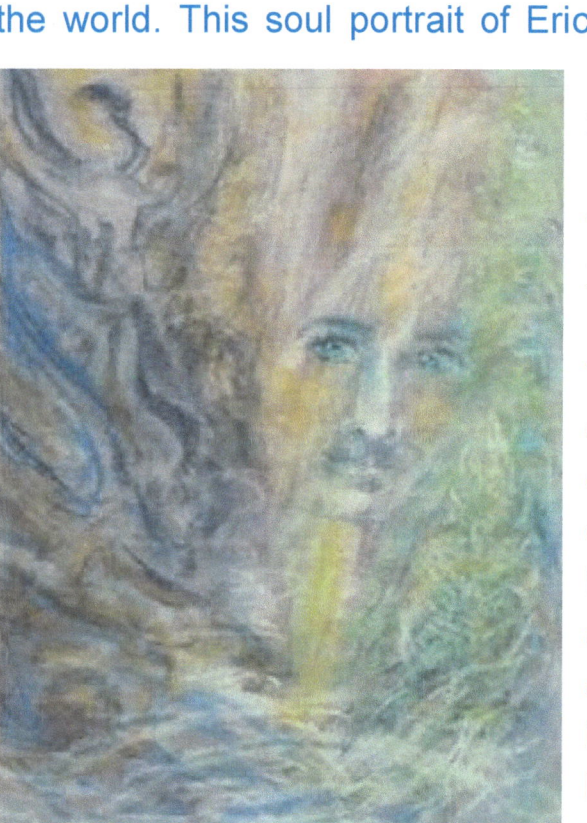

via photo in Vienna during my trip to Europe in 2011, when Eric had found himself at a crossroad.

The living interaction (resonance) with his channelled soul portrait and soul reading offered clarity, guidance, and a renewed connectedness with Divine source, increasing his self-confidence, empowering him to explore and enhance his extraordinary healing faculties and gifts of inspiration, streaming directly, information from the Divine Light. Soon after his soul portrait, Eric manifested the perfect workplace as a healer.

Short resume of Eric's testimonial:
Reconnection and Rebirth

"Una's channelled artistic and verbal expression revealed and explained, through color vibrations, the movements and information coming from my subtle energy bodies on the physical, emotional, mental and spiritual levels. It revealed my 'yet unrealized' potential, and the process of my personal evolution. I realized how my life experiences and changes were influenced by my inner states.

During the following weeks, awareness coming through my dreams, enlightening information from Una (the expert, guided by her heart), provided an unlimited ongoing communication with my inner Self, has prompted profound personal and professional changes and increased my self-confidence. I have received 'keys' which are, and always will be, a driving force for my personal and professional decisions and actions. Thank you Una, my spiritual Mother."

Addendum:

I have known Eric for fifteen years. We have been best friends ever since offering each other support during challenging times. I am forever grateful to Eric, my dear angel brother (yes he is an earth angel), who has saved my life taking me on magical healing journeys of light via airways of light and love between Bordeaux, France and Honolulu. The sound vibrations of his voice streaming words of wisdom, bliss, and healing directly from Source of Divine Light, ever uplifting, creating rainbows in our life, that you can sense in the soul portrait. Eric is, and always will be, an angel of peace.

This is a photo of my dear soul friend Eric and I in Bordeaux, France; my other heart homeland besides Austria and Hawaii.

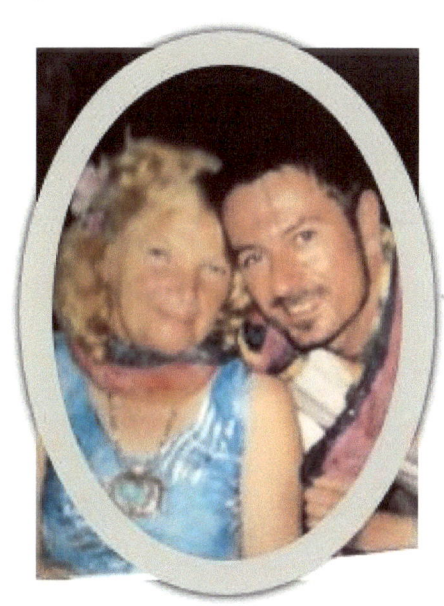

This friendship is bathed in eternal light filled with love and bliss. Remember, the power of Divine Light is like a diamond; unbreakable, shining through the thickest dark clouds, into all human hearts and minds, onto planet earth, into infinite universes and galaxies. Believe it!

SENDING JOY, BLISS, DANCING LIGHT AND PENNIES FROM HEAVEN,

FROM YOUR GRANDMA...

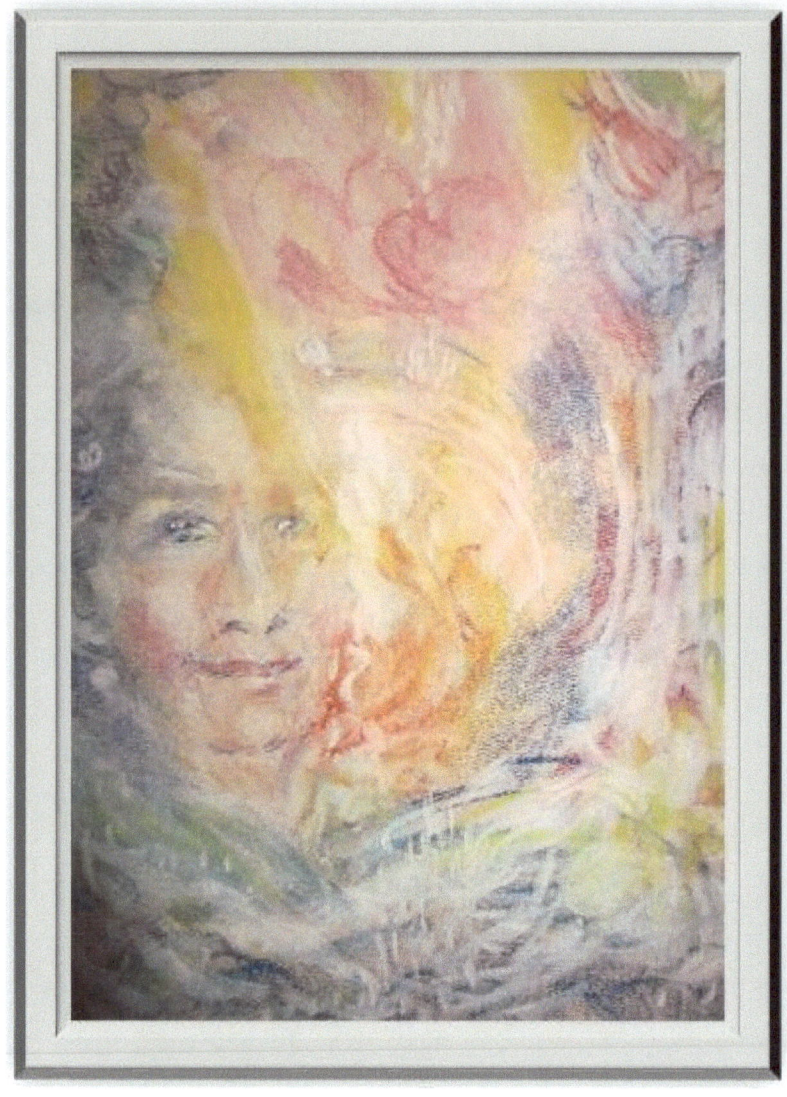

"To Una, I am overwhelmed with love and joy of the true heartfelt connection you have made with my dear departed grandma. You captured the essence of her heavenly youth with all the little pockets of messages that came through her spirit portrait, such as the pennies from heaven, that she shared with me as a little girl, and still does to this day, finding pennies throughout my day, especially in tough times as timely confirmations and signs from heaven on my journey. My grandma confirming the importance of our Angel Church; and so MANY, MANY MORE messages of light and love came through. My grandma is certainly one of my angels. My heart overflows, thank you, Una for the wonderful messages and truth, Much Love, Sundi"

It's important to know that our loved ones will always look after us and help us when we need it the most. Just trust and surrender and be open for miracles, there is always a penny for us, when we need it the most or expect it the least.

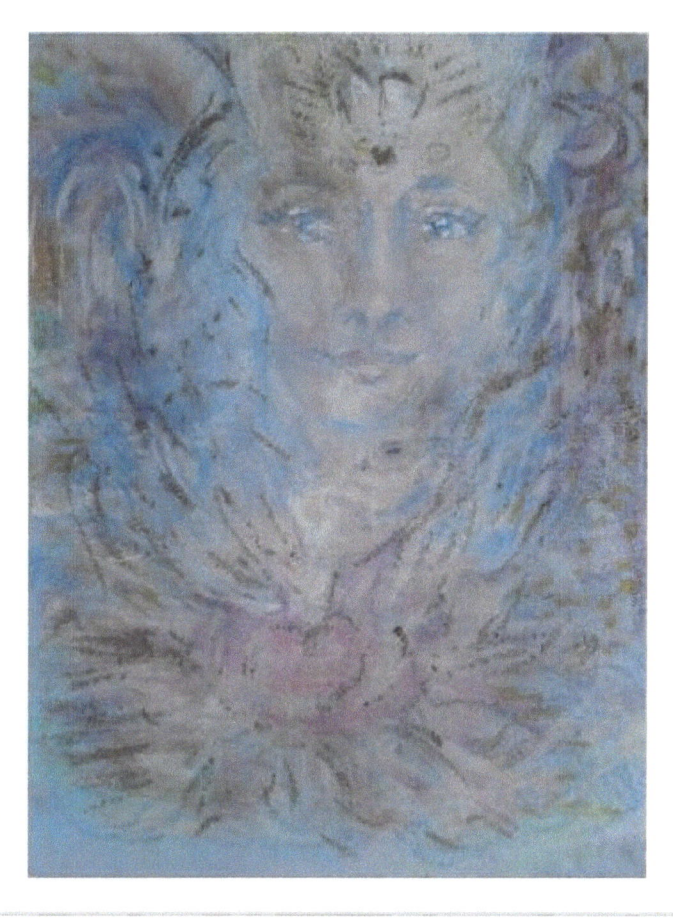

An angel looks at you and watches lovingly over you, sharing messages of wisdom from the Divine book of illumination. Sending thousands of blessings inviting you to surrender to the tender healing power of love. Sundi Sturgeon painted by Una White.

"My soul portrait allowed me to accept parts of myself, that I knew were there but I was afraid to express them because of my family. My soul portrait helped me to own those parts of myself, to see and understand myself. It's about validating and confirming my mission as a messenger of wisdom, healing and love from the angels, I realized that I channelled information from the angels, always coming through in a loving way, offering healing and bringing forth something that people may be missing from their childhood."

This soul portrait inspired and encouraged Sundi to claim her mission as an angelic messenger and healer, inspiring her to travel to Maui to be certified as angel reader/healer by Doreen Virtue. A power drawing in soft pastels following her soul portrait representing her beloved cat Charlie, a unique magical loving healer cat, confirming vividly the urgency to officially claim her mission as angel healer.

Sundi and Joey's couple soul portrait created on Maui in 2012, shows perfect harmony and total happiness between them and with Maui. Sharing the Christ consciousness is very important in their life, and life's work. Having co-created a healing center in a past life, their souls' desire to revive the healing gifts from the past inspired them to offer pioneering healing tools at their Holistic Light Rejuvenating Center in Sacramento. Called by "Mother" Maui to implement their center, Sundi and Joe moved to Maui. Maui brought them together for a common goal; to realize together their Divine purpose. As emissaries of the Elohims, guardians of the Hawaiian Islands, (Sundi is an earth angel sending messages from the book of wisdom), Sundi and Joe are assigned to work together with these angels, coming back during times of change to bring the light, raising consciousness by offering information and tools of light, to co-create transformation, renewal and planetary healing.

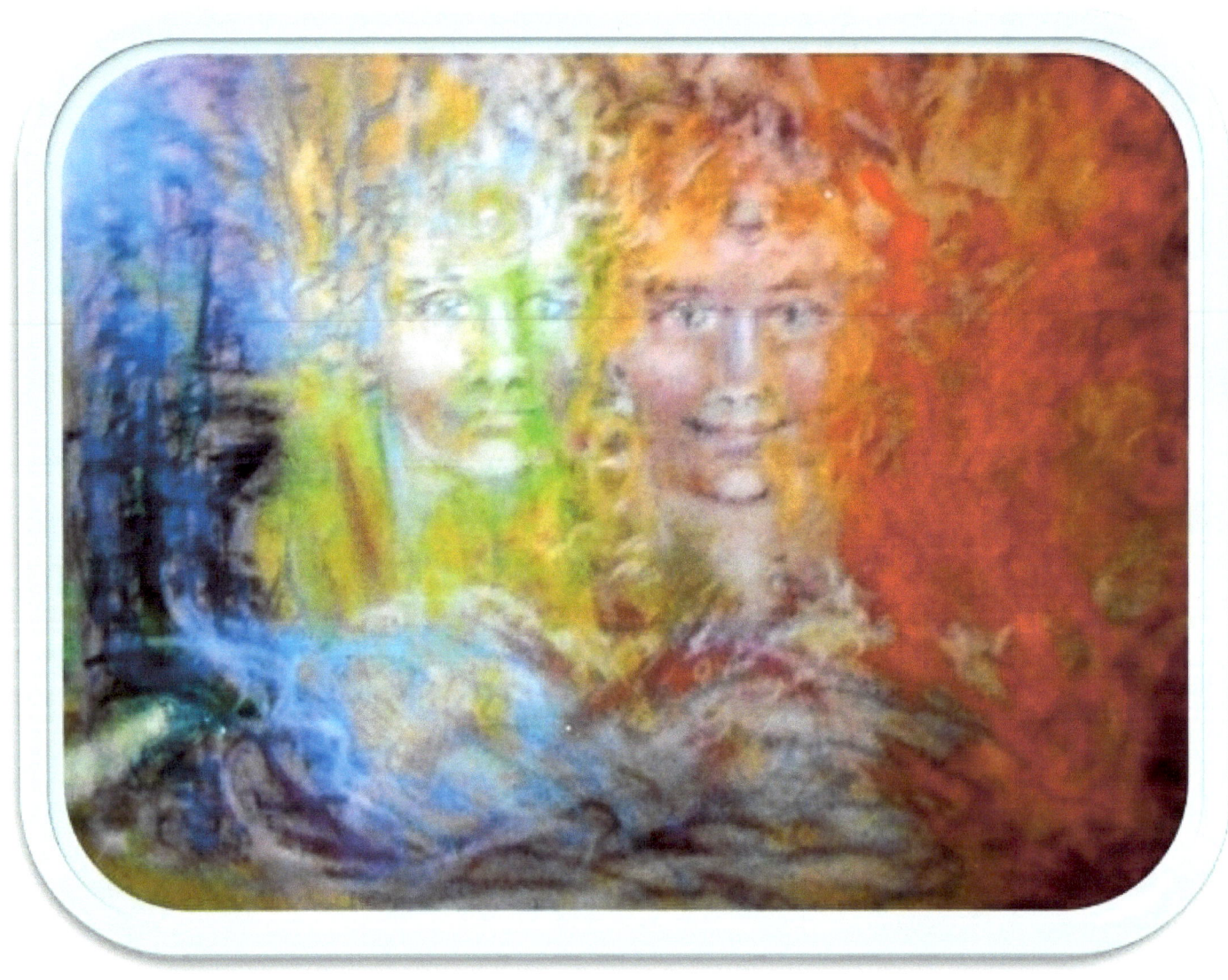

SOUL PORTRAITS OF PETS

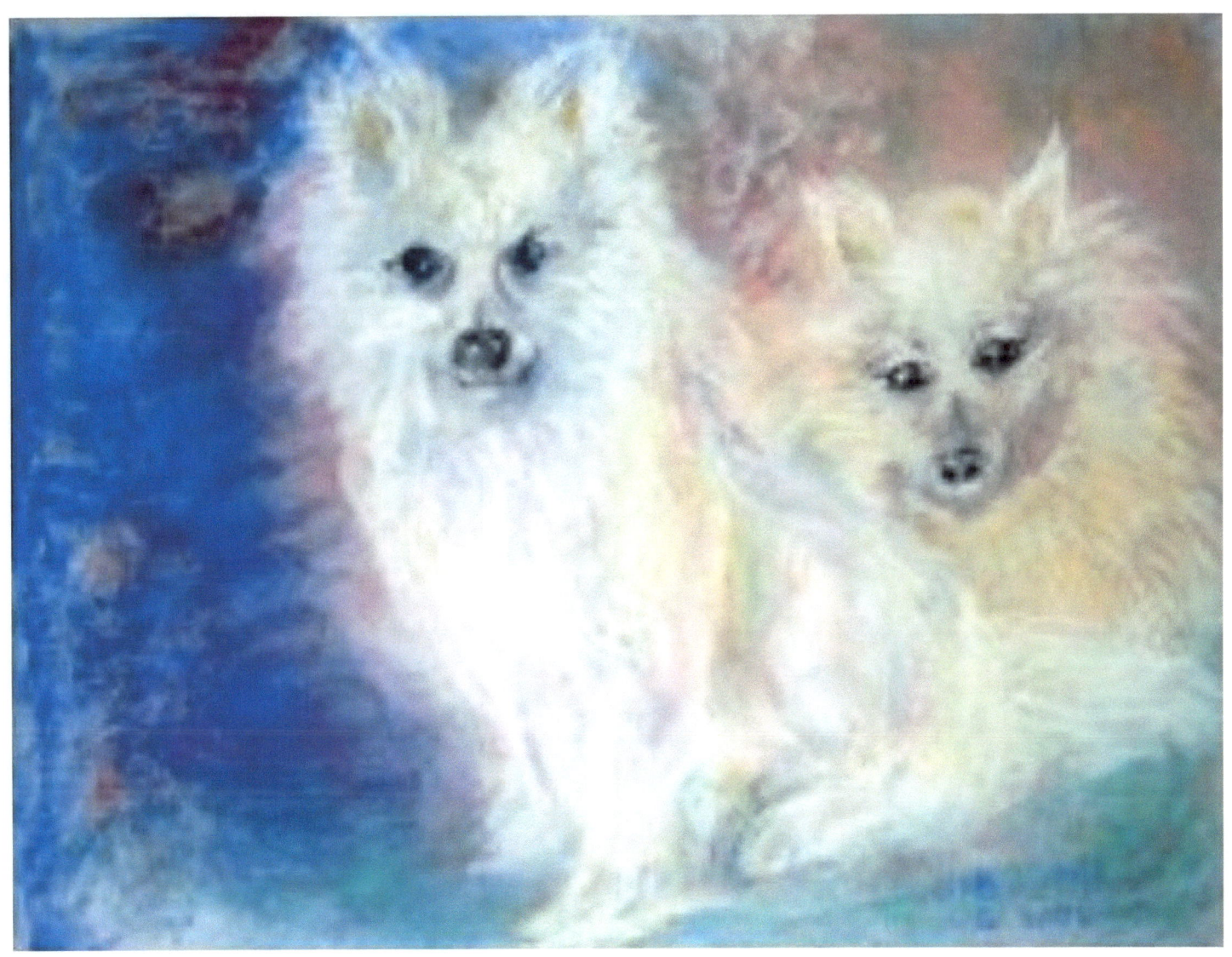

I have a passion to paint soul portraits of animals on earth and animals who passed away. Soul portraits of pets reveal their feelings, their true beautiful nature. Their soul and spirit continues to love and inspire us from the Other Side. Our pets keep in touch with us from their heavens, offering messages and insights to their beloved human friends.

Charlie the Mystic Healer Lover

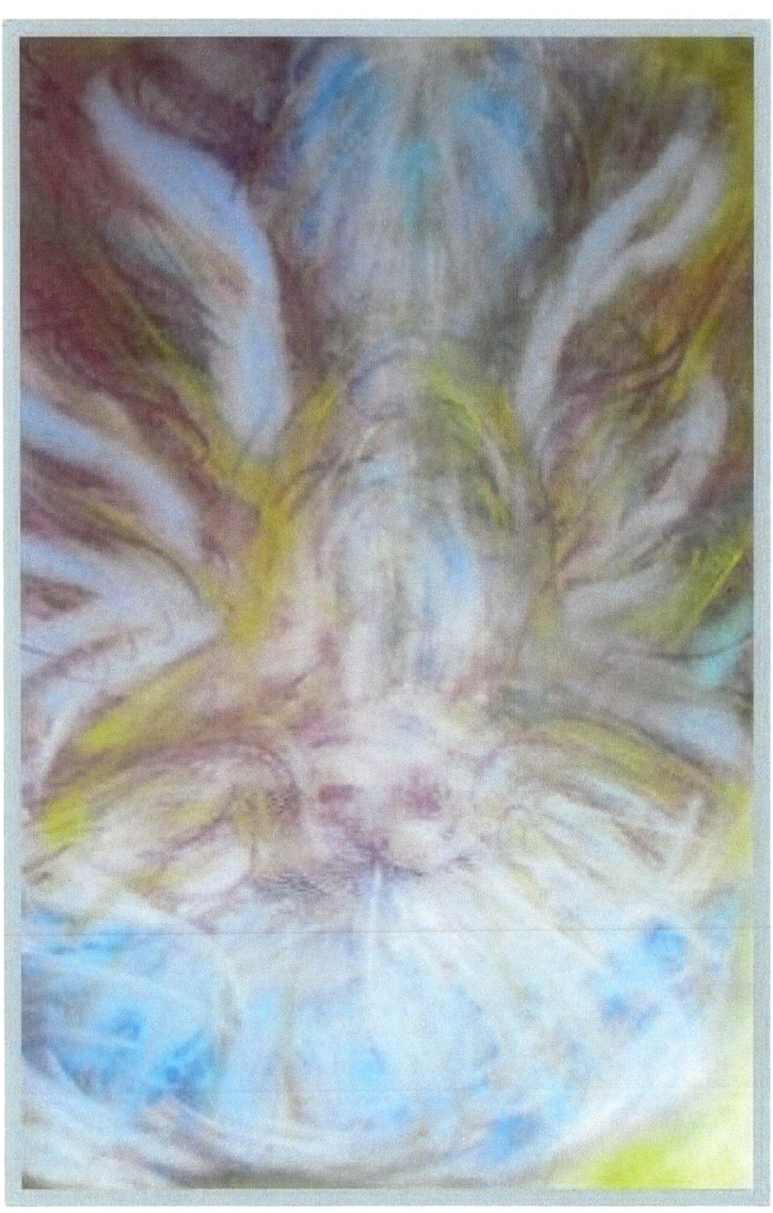

Charlie came to Denise one night, crawling right into the open hood of his car to make sure that Denise took him home. Always close and so tender with Joey and Sundi, Charlie radiated a loving, healing presence.

Charlie used to sit on my Tarot cards or under the table touching my colors, before I even started my work; his loving presence truly inspired my readings and soul portraits. One day my dear friends found him dead on the porch, a very shocking experience. Feeling his spirit, I immediately drew his soul portrait via a photo:

Soul Colors: **Greens**, **Pinks**, and **Purple**; colors representing healing, love, and mysticism. Archangels Metatron (bringer of the golden light and happiness), and Raphael the healer, were around him.

Charlie was emerging from a big pink heart from the kingdom of love. Charlie is a mystic and healer with shamanic gifts, a time traveller and loves music. Holding a blue heart in his paws, he is saying to you (Sundi and Joe); **"this is for you, just for you, I am offering you my blue heart from my heavens (Charlie's heavens), a big blue heart filled with kindness and peace is my gift to you, Sundi and Joey."**

Charlie says he is so sorry that he left so fast, so suddenly. He apologizes… when crossing the street, he was not paying attention, he was in another world; in a dream world. He thanks Sundi and Joey for all the care, love and appreciation.

"I AM ALWAYS HERE, I am looking out for you and I have never had a heaven on earth but with you, Sundi and Joey… smile when you think of me, smile when you work, when you play, I am with you. I paint with you…expressing tenderness, loyalty, peace and nobility. I talk to your heart through my eyes, saying I love you… I will be a communicator and an inspiration from beyond."

Charlie is capable of appearing in other paintings, when his spirit feels it is important:

He appeared in a power drawing I did for Sundi; representing a multitude of angel wings coming together with his face as a focal point, as the conductor of the angelic vehicle. This magical power painting of manifestation became a powerful inspiration for Sundi to claim and embody her mission as emissary of the Elohim angels; bringing messages of wisdom, hope and healing to all. Soon after this power painting, Sundi, Joe and I flew to Maui to be certified by Doreen Virtue as angel reader/healer.

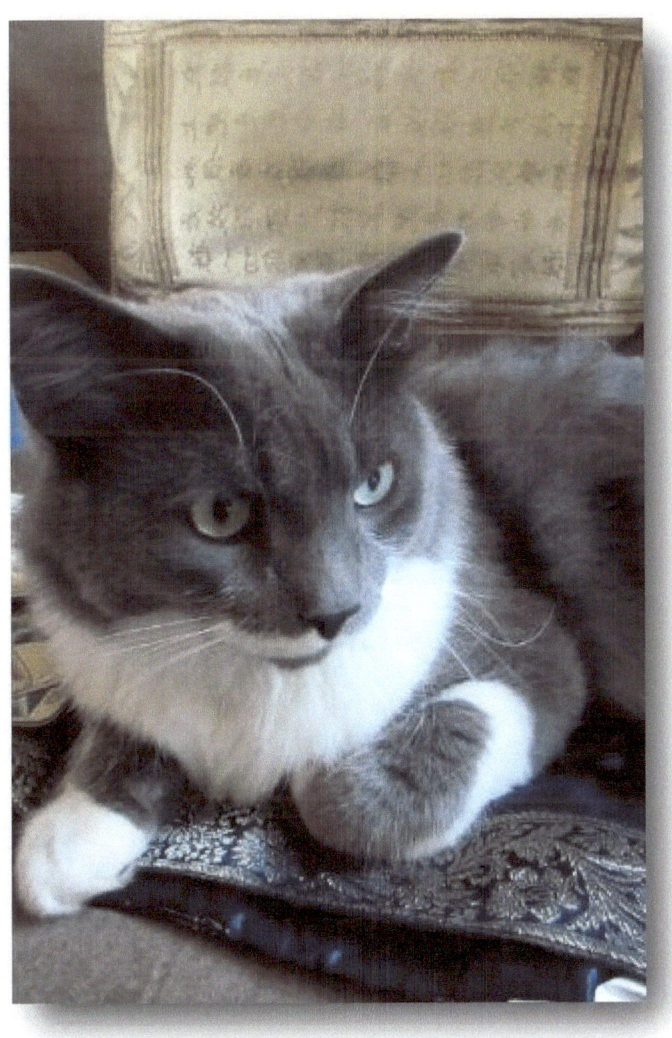
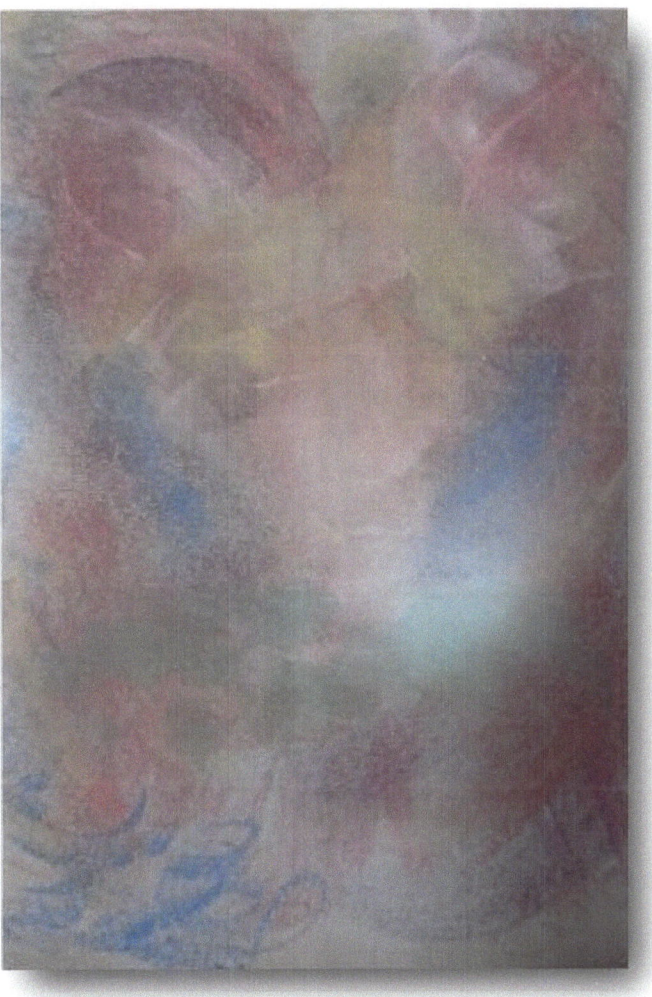

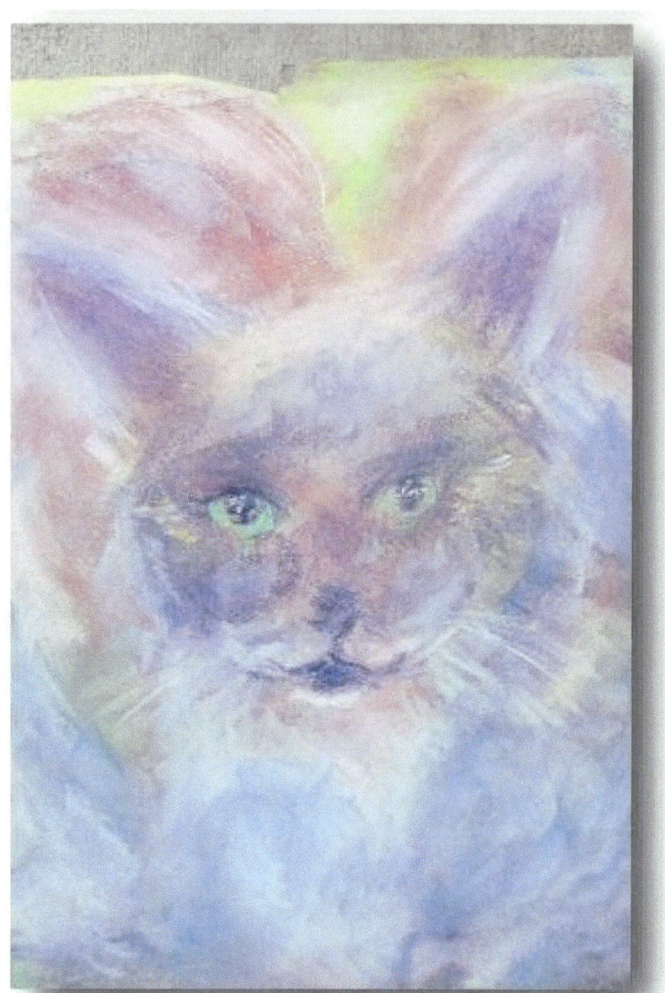
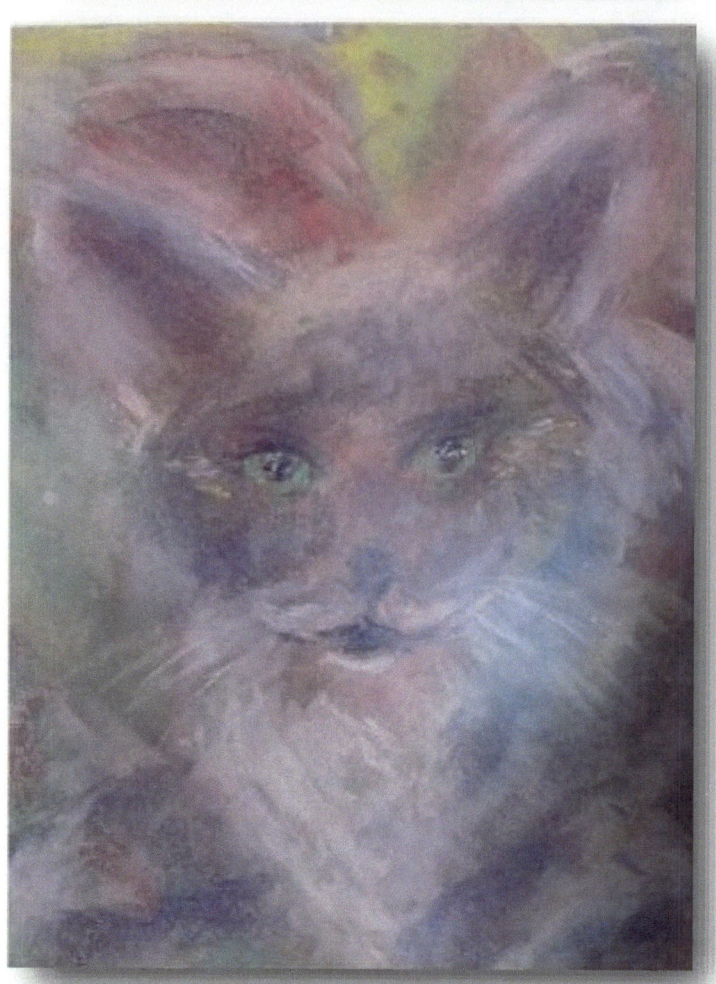

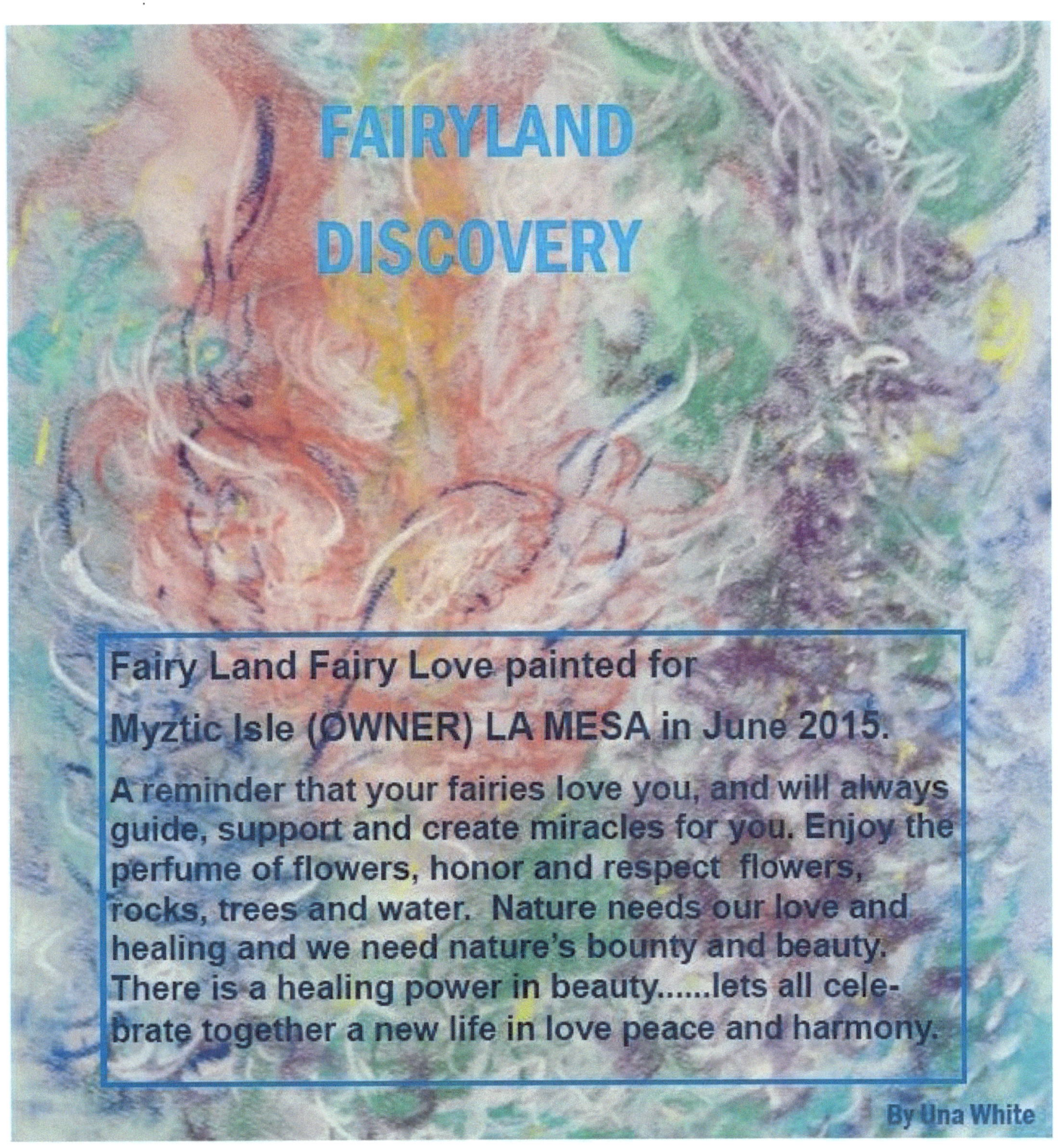

Stevie the Musician

From the desire to die to the desire to live, ignited by Una's soul portrait of Stevie, a life-saving experience.

His soul portrait has transformed his sense of hopelessness, re-awakening this passion and love of life, his create/musical talents.

This soul portrait of Stevie expresses the fullness of life energy and creativity, revealing and making his special gift of being mischievous and magical.

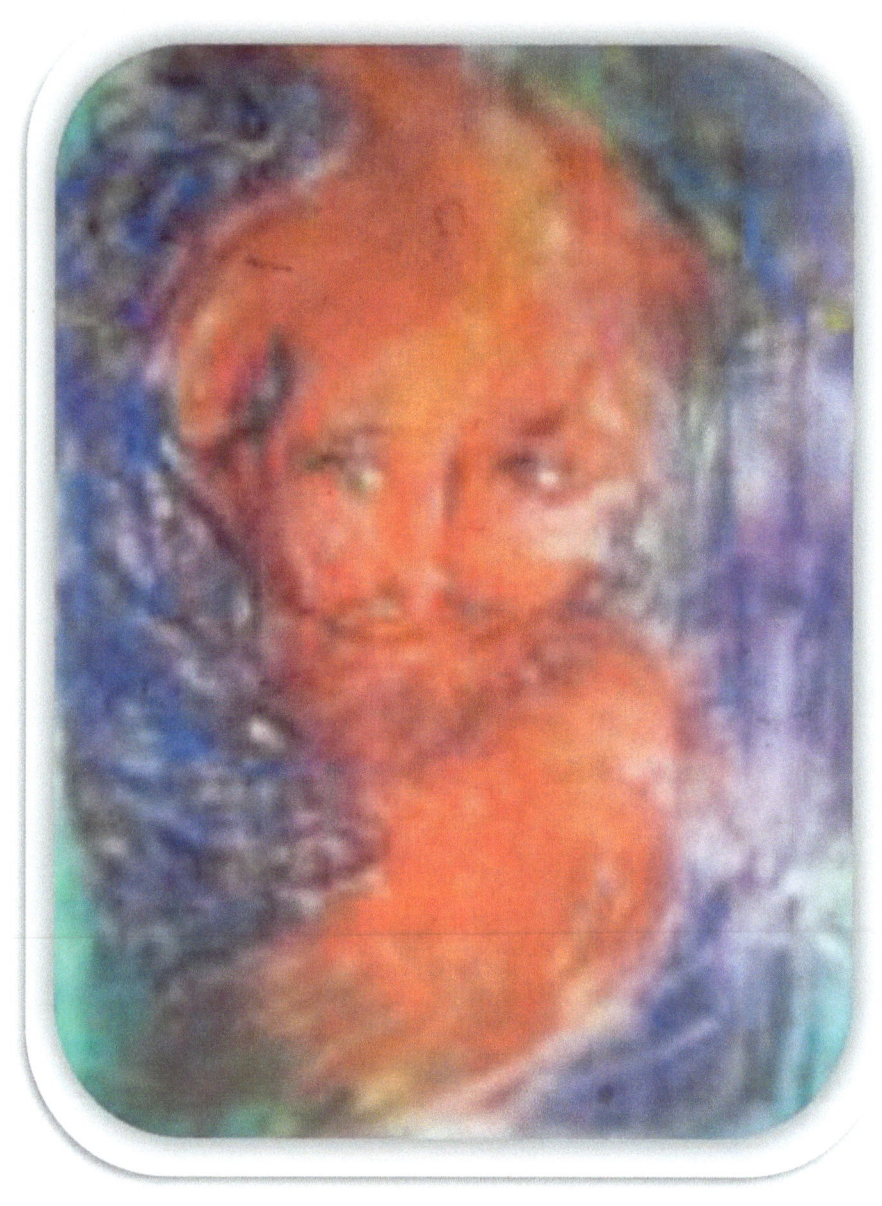

The sense of magic replacing a sense of powerlessness, uncovers our talents, and special qualities to overcome life-threatening situations and life's challenges.

Windwalker

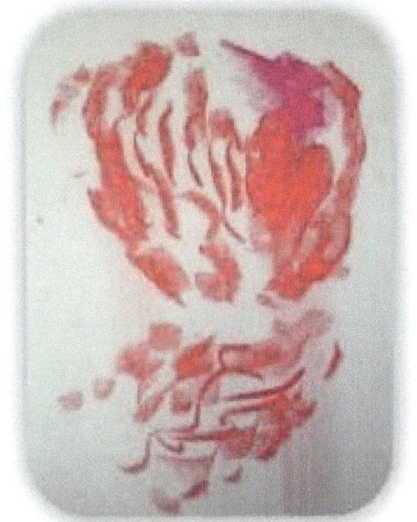
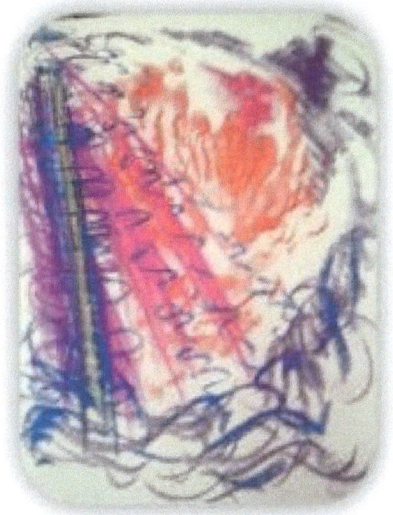
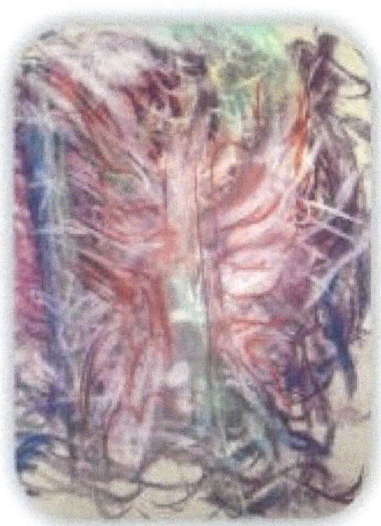

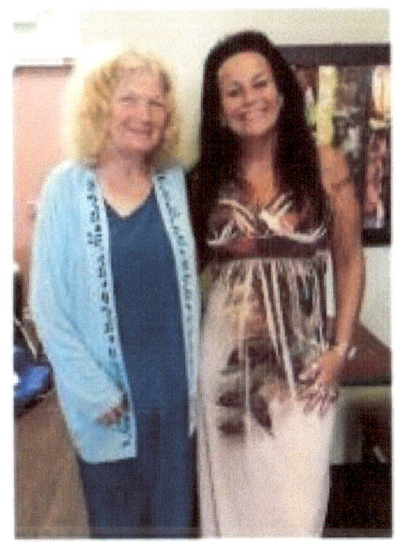

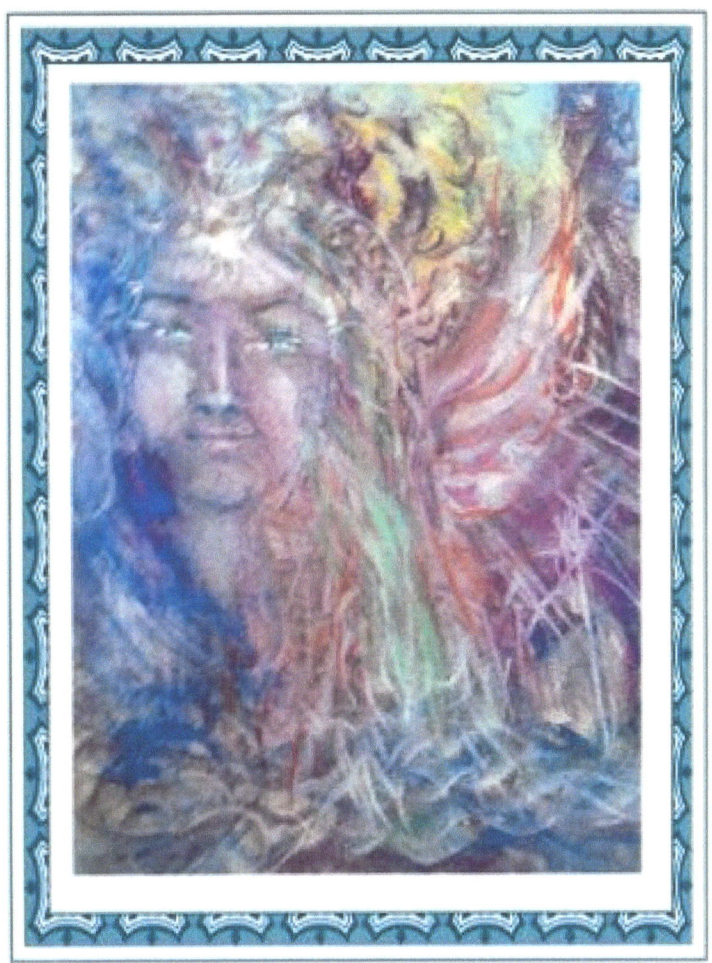

Windwalker
Native American
Nationally acclaimed
Shaman, Musician & Healer
won a Grammy music award

By Una White

Healing Power of Aura & Soul Portraits

Windwalker

This is windwalker's soul portrait which created the beginning of our friendship; a beautiful souls' connection. I always had great admiration and affinity with the Native American culture. Meeting Windwalker was an incredible gift in my life. We offered together a workshop, blending European and Native American shamanic techniques. More workshops are planned.

Windwalker's soul portrait reveals:

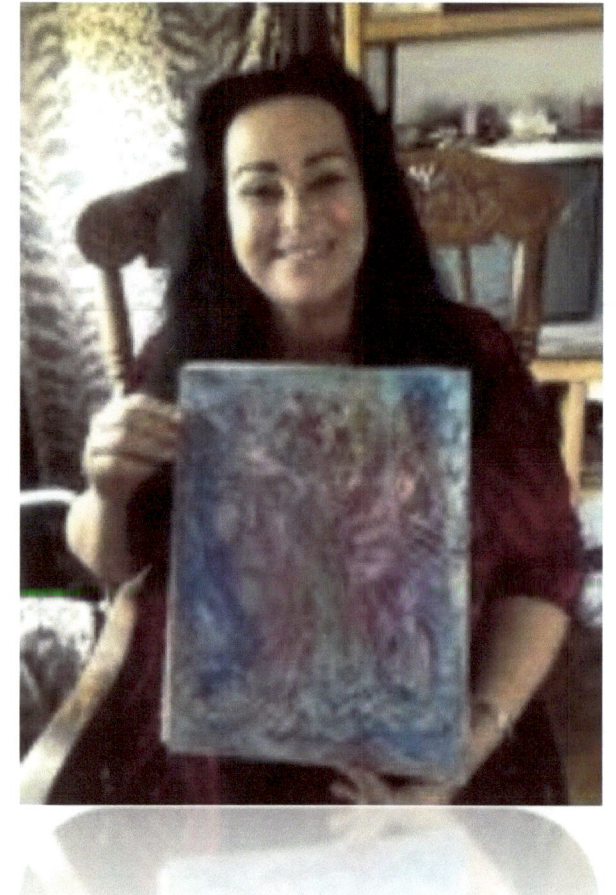

HER AMAZING FIRE OF CREATIVITY AND PASSION FOR LIFE, her luminous, magical beauty, her mystical knowledge, extraordinary shamanic, healing and musical gifts (healing the waters). It's a testimonial of how the active creative power of the universe, all the elements and her ancestors are working through and with her in perfect one-ness and harmony. As a teacher, she expresses and shares a synthesis of all cultures, and dimensions offering timeless inspiration and healing.

The nurturing support by the spirit of a tree, other nature spirit friends, the elements (reminding her of her deep connection with nature), the animals, and her ancestors, offered her the strength to face and overcome successfully life's challenges and to move gracefully into new beginnings, emerging transformed, more beautiful, triumphant and powerful than ever. Windwalker keeps being celebrated and honoured nationally through musical awards for her heart-moving, transformational shamanic healing work.

Windwalker's testimonial:

"The powers of the universe surround us, as they gather us together, for the bigger and mystical answers we all have, and that are needed. Thank you Una for all that you are, and are becoming. Warruishi, for showing me who I am and for loving me. You are truly amazing. May your path be blessed."

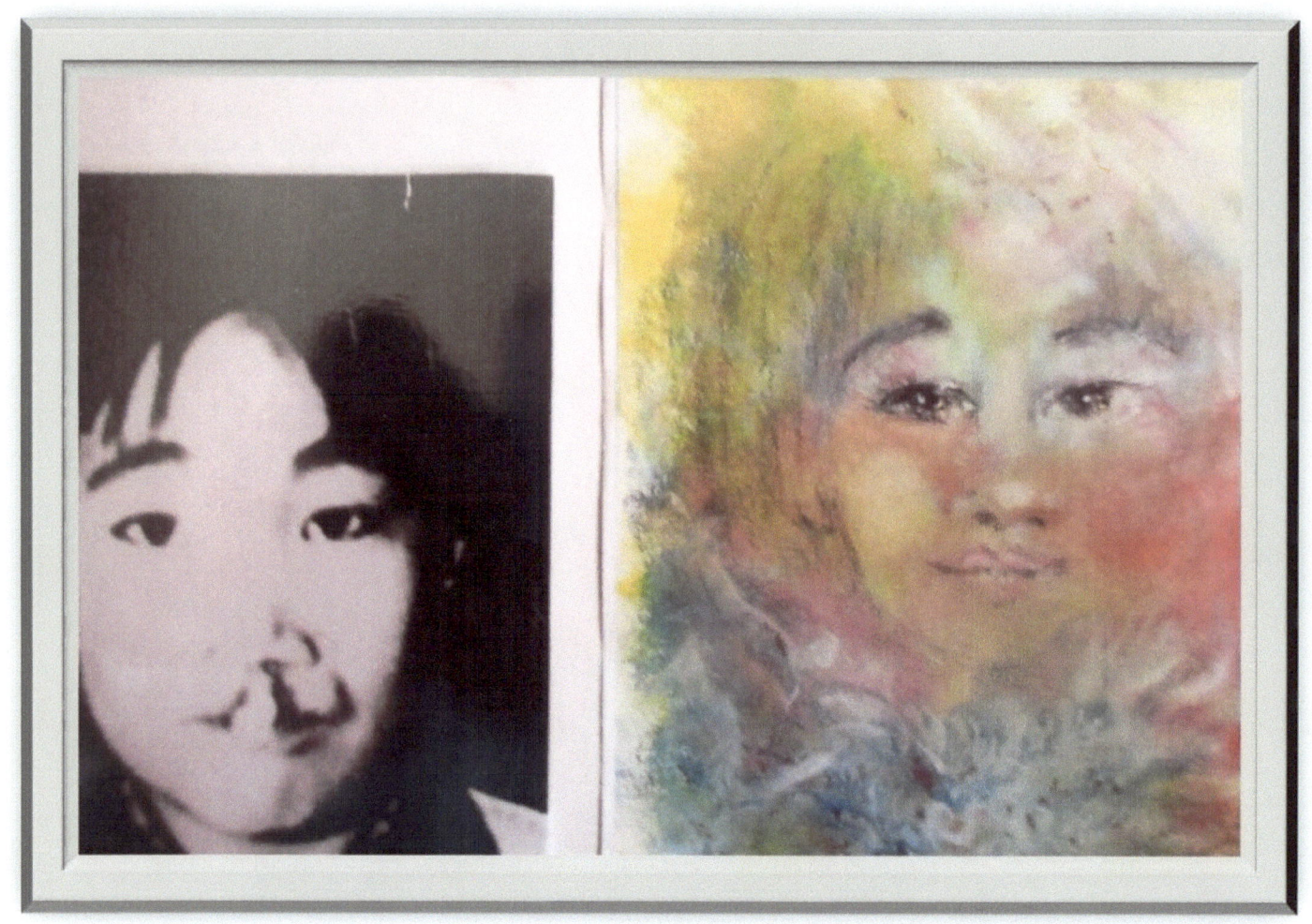

HEALING POWER OF BEAUTY

Soul portrait of a Chinese girl with deformed pallet before surgery,. Commissioned by the Smile Train Organization, so she could look forward to being healed and enjoy her radiant beauty and love herself. The Smile Train Organization's surgeons are offering free surgery worldwide to kids correcting the mouth area.

Divine beauty is not always what you see right away, as you may be distracted by exterior appearances, deformities, etc. The light of the soul shining from a person's eyes can erase a thousand wrinkles…and make us smile. True beauty comes from within…we are reminded to be aware, connect with and radiate our unique Divine Light and beauty the sparkle of Divine consciousness.

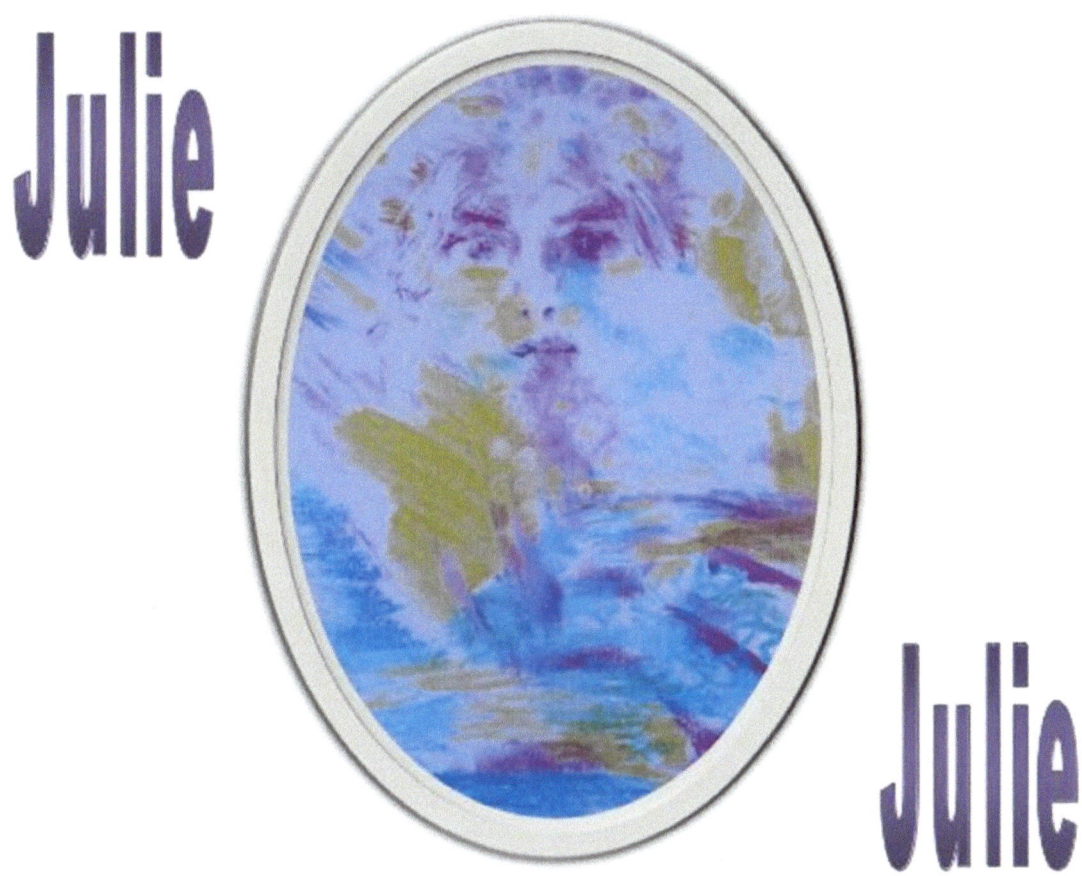

Angel of Music…Experiencing the Angel of Music Within

Julie is in touch, talking with the angels every day, but only when she is alone, she is telling me as I draw her angelic soul portrait, representing angelic vibrations, angels in different colored robes. She draws, at the same time, without knowing which colors I am using, an angelic picture with the same colors. She talks about her special relationship with the angels, feeling totally part of the angelic world.

She experiences herself as a fairy, an angel, a magician with magical gifts of peace, harmony, healing and music. This soul portrait represents a little angelic girl, looking from heaven down on earth: gentle, full of generosity, being and bringing the sun light to all the people. Thus the angelic world is peacefully integrated in her every day life. She continuously expresses her joy of communicating with the angels, as part of her everyday life. How many children dream of revealing and communicating their wonderful encounters with the angels, and are afraid not to be misunderstood. For them the angels are as real as we are. Let's encourage these natural gifts to unfold instead of suppressing them. How often our children are our most wondrous teachers.

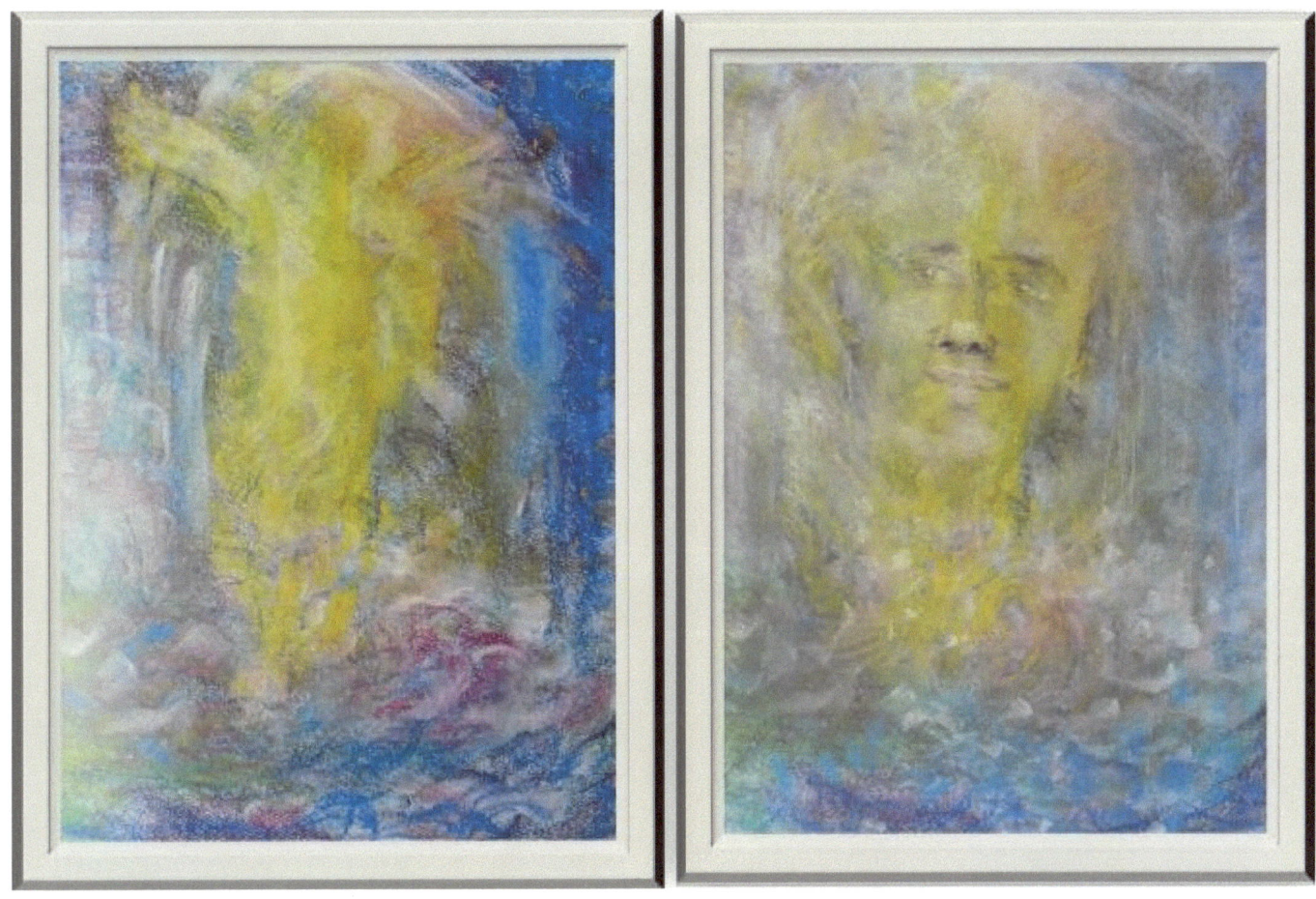

Patrick died in Iraq, now he is his mom's guardian angel. Patrick is forever protecting her, giving her the energies of strength during moments of vulnerability. He is proud of his mom and her work dedicated to the well-being of veterans. *"They need all the attention, respect, care and healing."*

Communicating his qualities and energies of his triumphant spirit, perseverance, strength, and love to his mom.

It is my heart's desire to promote permanent peace amongst us and on earth, by raising the awareness of fighting unnecessary wars, causing unnecessary suffering and death for so many…How many more lives will be wasted in vain. May global peace become part of the new Divinely inspired humanity.

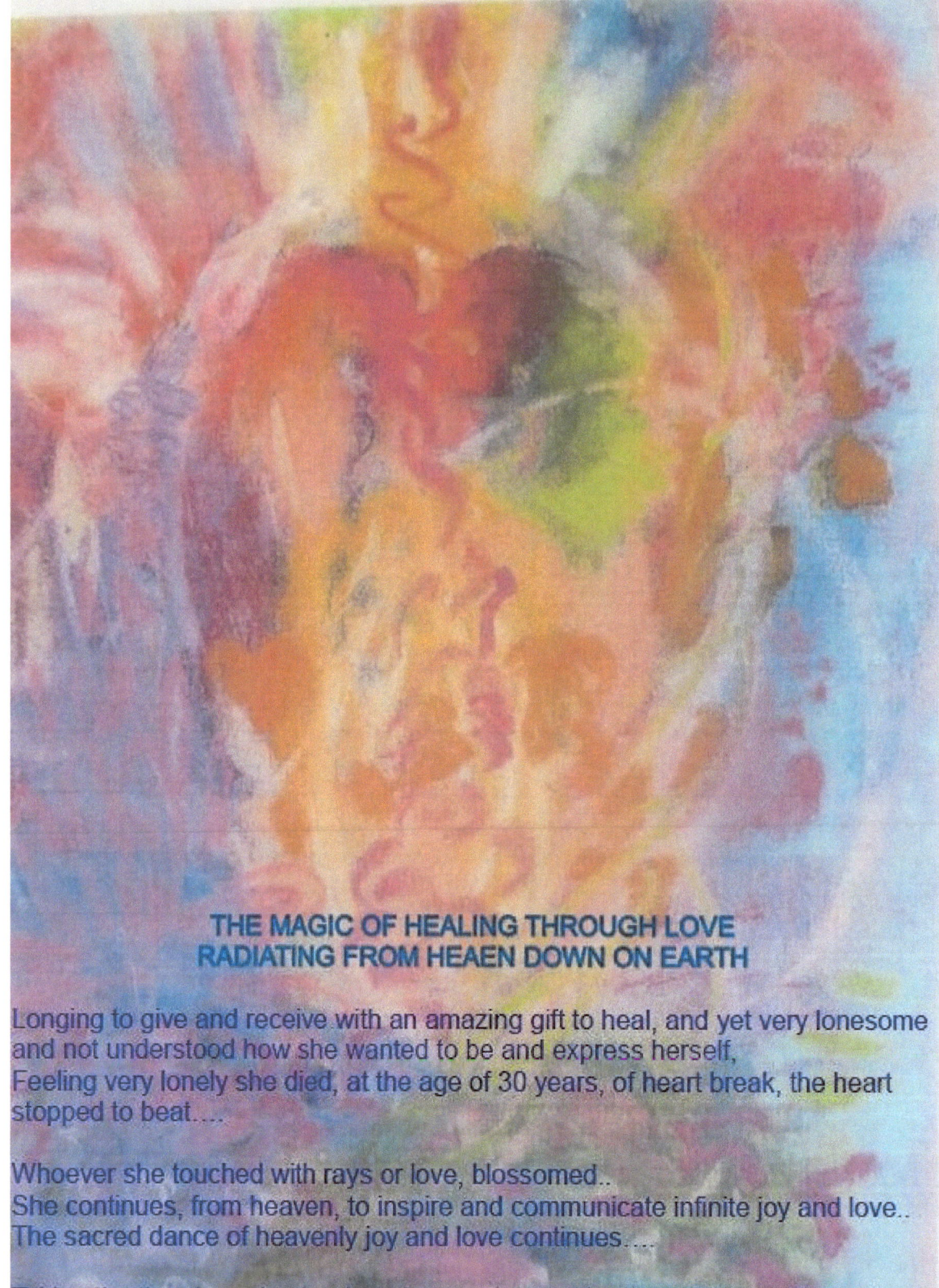

**THE MAGIC OF HEALING THROUGH LOVE
RADIATING FROM HEAEN DOWN ON EARTH**

Longing to give and receive with an amazing gift to heal, and yet very lonesome and not understood how she wanted to be and express herself,
Feeling very lonely she died, at the age of 30 years, of heart break, the heart stopped to beat….

Whoever she touched with rays or love, blossomed..
She continues, from heaven, to inspire and communicate infinite joy and love..
The sacred dance of heavenly joy and love continues….

Taking the time to understand and appreciate each other with our gifts and unique qualities, and what we wish to share, and just enjoy the quality of true heart felt communication, is more essential than ever during these times of cell phone, texting etc…….

Una White

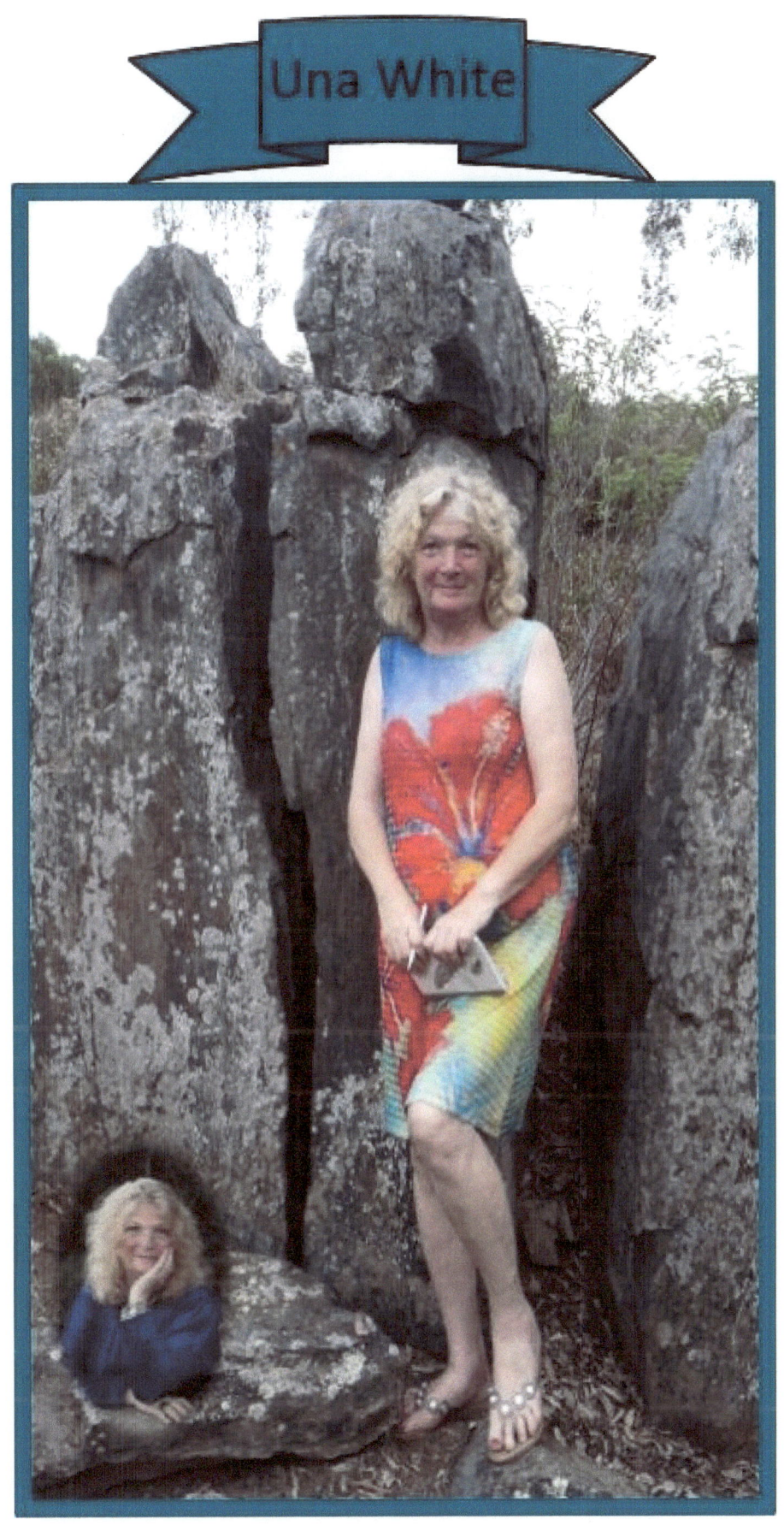

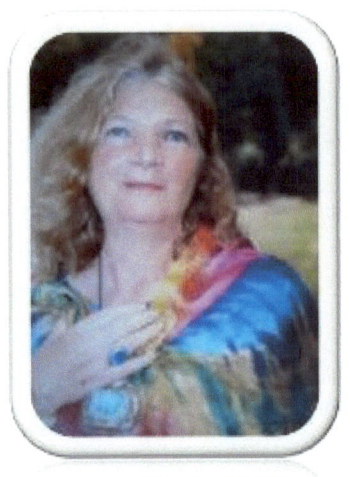

ITS ALL ABOUT LOVE

WHEN THE POWER OF LOVE OVERCOMES THE LOVE OF POWER, THERE WILL BE PEACE FOR EVER

Love transmutes, transform, heals, unites
Love fills everything, every cell of our body/mind/soul

Love restores all that is to its natural state of Divine perfection. If we just listen to our heart, letting go of control, fear or any barriers,….

And gratefully accept the gift of grace with its many faces

By Una White, artistic medium/transpersonal art therapist, relationship mentor

See Section 11 for all about Una's Work

www.unaarthealinglight.com

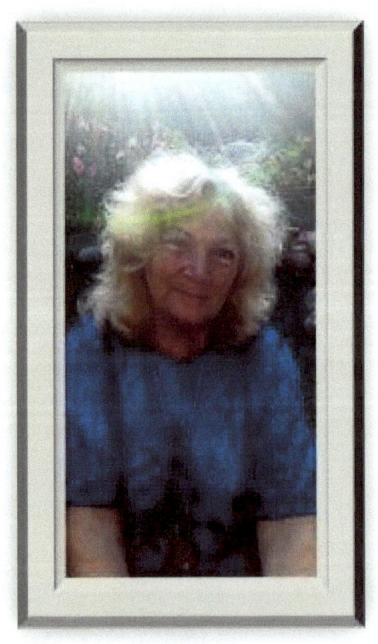

HEALING POWER OF AURA & SOUL PORTRAITS

PART II

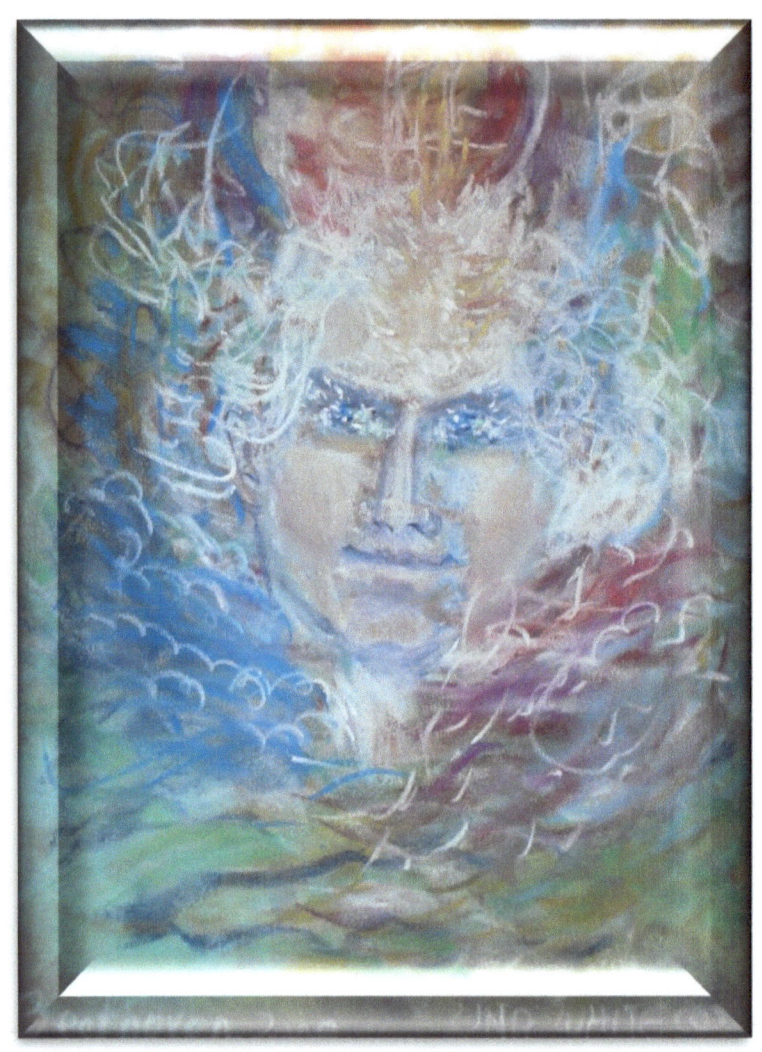

LUDWIG VAN BEETHOVEN 1770 - 1827

A true visionary, deeply spiritual, mystical and very passionate. Gifted with Divine wisdom, inspiration and knowledge, it's his deepest heart desire to help mankind evolve to a new and higher level of consciousness and higher dimensions. Through his music he saw himself as a prophet, a seer, a lover of nature, viewing music as sacred.

A CHALICE IN WHITE, YELLOW AND ORANGE, REPRESENTING THE POWER OF THE DIVINE PRESENCE AND INSPIRATION, THE FIRE OF CREATIVITY AND PASSION. On the crown chakra; the portal to God, in gold, is wide open and receiving heavenly music. Sometimes he was overwhelmed by all those melodies moving his soul and spirit, inspiring him, living in him. The white spirals represent vibrations of Divine energies, movements, the triumphant power of Spirit, and the muses; an ecstatic dance of the spirits, all embracing,

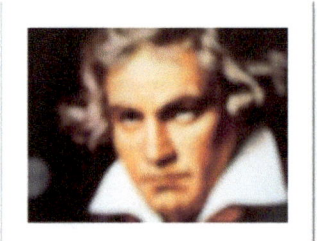

guiding, inspiring him lovingly to create his magnificent music. Heavenly music in all forms, represented in different color vibrations. Tremendous passion, a sense of victory, the triumphant spirit over any limitations is manifest in his music.

GREEN: represents his love of nature,. He loves the Wienerwald, that's where he felt most at home and where he composed the Pastorale, the 6th symphony. *"I am feeling in harmony, no matter what is happening around me, when I am in nature, especially in the lovely meadows and forests of the Kahlenberg."*

Imagine Beethoven walking barefoot in the meadows, in the hills of the Wienerwald, where he found peace, listening to the spirits of the trees, flowers, rocks, water, the wind and the sun talking, flirting, and singing to him inspiring him to transpose his experiences into his delightful music...

"In the woods I am blessed, even trees speak to me, I love the waves of harmony, emanating from the green meadows. I am feeling happy, passionate, and an ecstatic power is overwhelming me with celestial harmonious melodies flowing into me, it's an invitation and inspiration to create victory of light over dark, of good over evil. My music empowers victory, my music is a manifestation and celebration of God's music; forever resonating in all the universes witnessing the unlimited power of God, for ever. We are all one, in our bodies, souls and spirits, we are all accepted in the oneness of God. Experiencing the power of the sunrise and sunset has always ignited the fire of my music "

At first I drew an expression of bitterness, and anger, but gradually the expression of excitement of victory over our human limiting conditions took over. Beethoven is feeling very beautiful, powerful, and happy in the portrait, like a young man, enjoying the presence of his loving messengers from the cosmos (DARK BLUE), nature and the Light. The portrait is showing his face totally surrounded by swirling Divine energies, in total bliss, listening, with his eyes, ears and heart wide open, as he receives heavenly images and music, bringing heaven and earth and the whole universe together through music creating peace and harmony for ever.

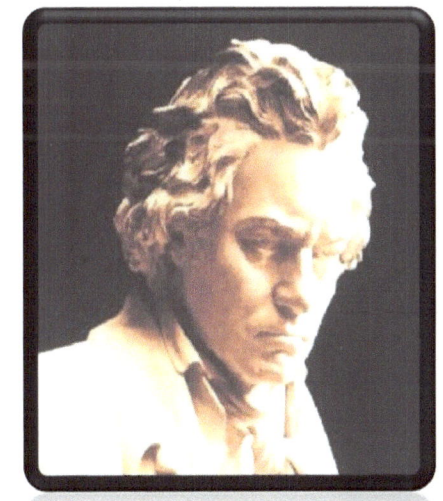

HIS MESSAGE TO US:

"My work of music is to celebrate the glory of God, to ignite the sparkle of the Divine within all of us, and to create infinite joy, peace, and harmony. Don't ever give up, follow and trust the power, support and guidance of the Divine within, open yourself to the wisdom from the cosmos, the universe, and nature. Nature is our foundation. We need nature as nature needs us. Explore and open yourself to the fire of creativity, it is endless. Believe in the unlimited power of harmony, in our body/mind/soul, and in our environment, this is what supports, and carries us. May the power of God's music celebrate the victory of the LIGHT over DARKNESS, raising global consciousness, ending all conflict by creating HARMONY and PEACE forever through MUSIC."

The ninth symphony enjoys still today a global political impact since its first performance in 1824, for instance, to celebrate the fall of the Berlin wall. In the ninth symphony, Beethoven mixes strong accents of despair and disillusionment, even outright terror, and balances these emotions with musical acts of overcoming, noble and life-affirming artistic creation, and, at times, joy. Within the anguish of his life and music there is Beethoven's *amor fati* - the love of his fate - and a stoicism that accompanies acceptance of whatever life might bring. In the midst of his crisis he said about his increasing deafness:

" *I will seize fate by the throat, it shall certainly not bend and crush me completely."*

Beethoven drew his last breath during a thunder and lightning storm.

Driven to fulfil his Divine destiny, Beethoven's power of music orchestrated by mighty Divine creative energies, combined with perseverance and determination, is a testimonial for the victory of his music, over all earthly concerns, dramas, pains, and even impulse of suicide (over his deafness), erased temporarily. Liberty was very important for Beethoven. His soul was filled with great love for humanity despite his deafness.

Some quotes by Beethoven:

"Art is a savior. In times of despair, true art walks hand in hand with nature. True art is imperishable.

"LIFE IS SHORT, ART IS ETERNAL. Life is becoming a sanctuary for art."

"IT IS IMPOSSIBLE TO LEAVE THIS WORLD UNTIL I HAVE PRODUCED ALL THAT I FELT CALLED UPON TO CREATE. I MUST LEAVE BEHIND ME ALL THAT SPIRIT HAS INSPIRED AND COMMANDED TO BE FINISHED."

I was guided to give his soul portrait a 'make over' after 7 years: It is showing his romantic, softer side; ILLUMINATION, ECSTASY, ODE TO JOY, IN GOD.

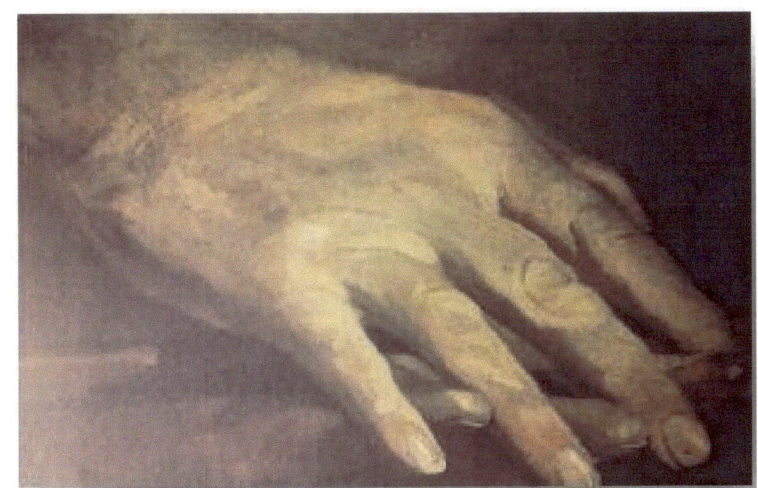 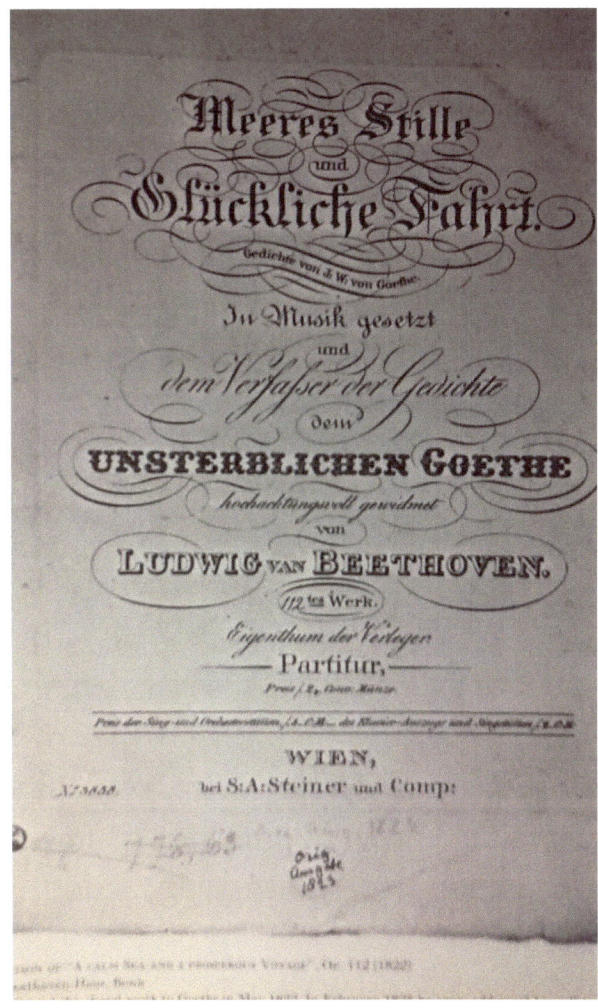

BRUNO GROENING
SOUL PORTRAIT PAINTED IN HONOLULU. QUOTES AND STREAMED INFORMATIONS BY UNA WHITE

SOUL COLORS: WHITE PURE DIVINE SPIRIT, DIVINE PRESENCE, ONENESS WITH THE DIVINE PRESENCE, LIGHT, HEALING POWER AND WISDOM

RED PURE LOVE, CREATIVITY, LIFE POWER AND LIFE ENERGY
An angelic being, from a rainbow temple, flying down to incarnate and bring love, and healing to all, GREEN healing gifts

This is the soul portrait of a very famous miracle healer, Bruno Groening from Germany, who died in Paris in 1955. Totally dedicated to his sacred healing ministry, his service to God, no matter the challenging situations he had to endure, Bruno has never given up his faith and belief in the unlimited healing stream of God working through him, healing thousands.

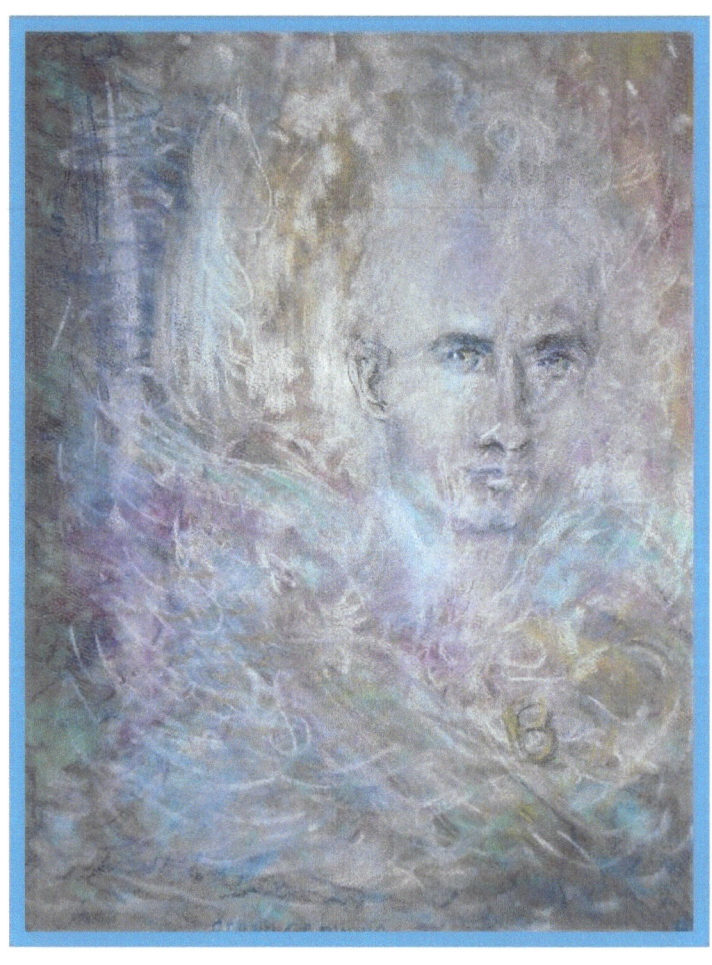

Direct vessel for the Divine, " I RE-ESTABLISH THE BRIDGE TO GOD, SO THAT YOU RECEIVE DIRECTLY THE DIVINE HEALING STREAM FLOWING INTO YOUR BODY, MIND, HEART AND SOUL.

Bruno insisted on the necessity of dissolving any negativity as an essential condition for promoting the healing process:

GOD'S HEALING ENERGY STREAMING INTO YOUR BODY ONLY WORKS IF THERE IS NO NEGATIVITY, IF YOU BELIEVE, HAVE FAITH IN GOD'S HEALING POWER AND SURRENDER COMPLETELY. THERE MAY BE A HEALING CRISIS BEFORE COMPLETE HEALING OCCURS. BELIEVE IN GOD AND GOD WILL HELP YOU. WHOEVER

DEDICATES HIS LIFE AND LIFE'S MISSION TO GOD, WILL ALWAYS ENJOY HIS SUPPORT AND PROTECTION.

Treated by the medical establishment in Germany with hatred, injustice, jealousy, emotional, mental abuse and more, Bruno has sacrificed his life and own health for the sake of truth and healing. He died in Paris from cancer.

During his lifetime, the 'Circle of Friends' was created by people in search of healing or simply to remember and celebrate Bruno: His healing energy is still active today in the circles of friends around the globe. People attuned to Bruno's spirit; 'creating a bridge to God', may experience Divine healing streaming directly from the Divine through Bruno into their body, wherever needed.

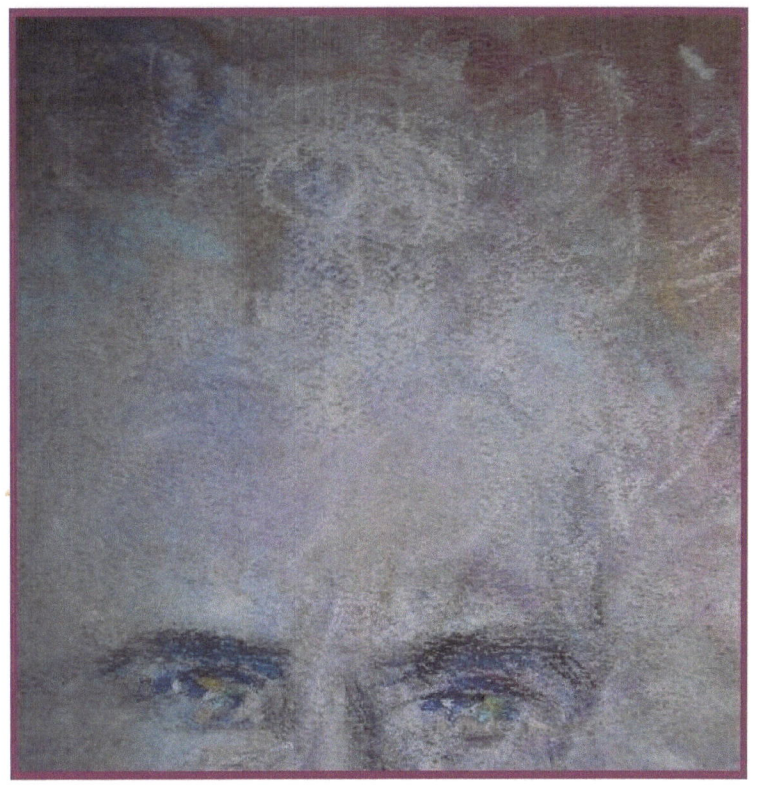

Bruno's eyes are the window to the soul

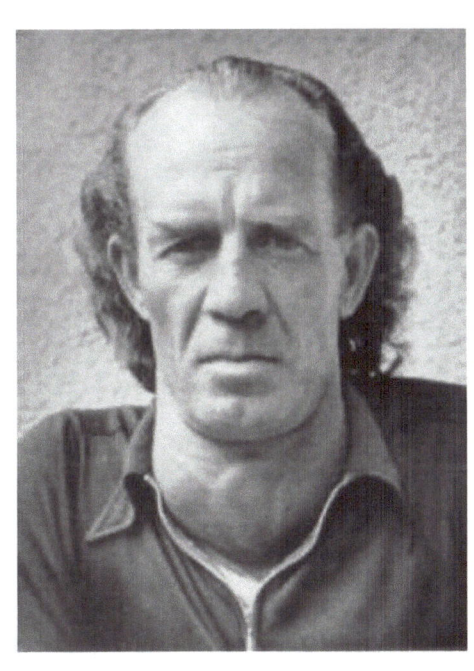

HEALING ENERGIES MAY MOVE AND TOUCH US BEYOND SPACE AND TIME, IF WE LOVINGLY AND HUMBLY CONNECT, OPEN OUR HEART AND ASK FOR HELP.

Bruno was aware of his constant unity with God: *"In God we are all one. I have not suffered in vain. Why was I born in Germany? I love France. I have not expressed my anger. I love my wife, I love Paris. I was too attached to the hope that I was finally recognized, instead I was betrayed and judged and condemned by the medical establishment in Germany. But I persevered until I gave the last drop of my life.*

I accepted wholeheartedly my faith, my service to God, I never gave up my path of service and healing Joy and gratitude to God, my wife, and the gifts God gave me. It is important to release any karmic bondage, to achieve true freedom. It is time for the karma of humanity to be transformed; Let true love enter your heart. Be love and know the truth, spoken to you by God, residing within your heart. To be in love with life is life saving for all intention to heal is essential.

Earth, nature, are important. Nature is sacred. Let children grow naturally. Balance within your heart and spirit is the key, Cosmic order must be restored for all.

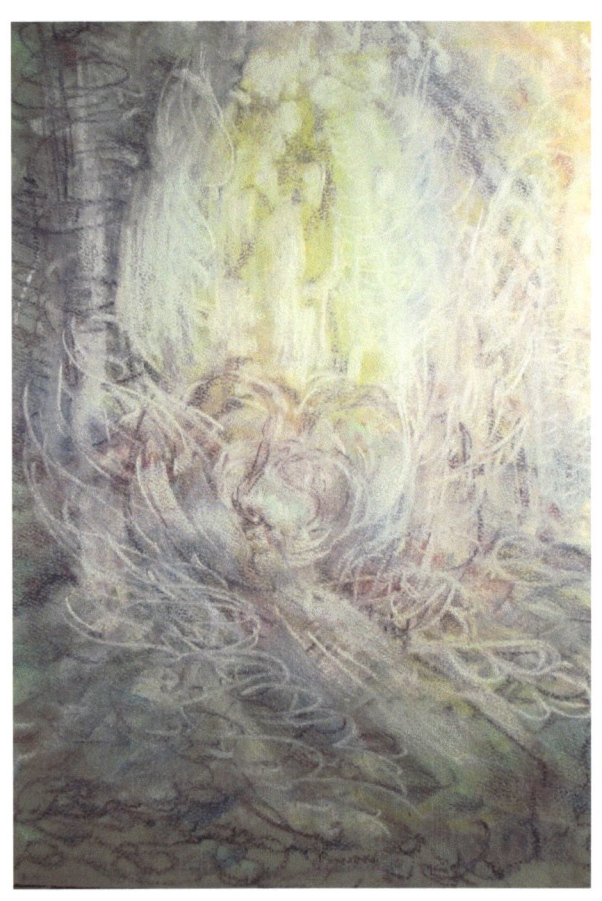

Nurture the flame of the Divine Spirit, the flame of your soul. Do not ever sacrifice the sacred life of your soul. Its expression and purpose is God's calling. If the soul is and stays crippled, it may finally perish; prevented from expressing its aliveness, its unique beautiful love, light and Divine gifts. Free your soul, let it talk to you, feel God's love as you listen to your soul. My journey into the light is a new beginning. Believe in the light. in the birth of light, believe in the creative force of God, in the Holy Spirit- Nurture the flame of the Divine Spirit."

The first drawing reveals Bruno's journey into the world of Divine Light, arriving through a sacred heart (red) in a landscape filled with golden and white Divine Light, Received by sacred masters, angelic beings and the creator, he is initiated into a high position as spiritual master/healer with gifts to continue streaming Divine healing light to those in need, from above.

BRUNO'S HEROIC LIFE 'S JOURNEY CAN SERVE AS A WARNING: HISTORY MUST NOT REPEAT ITSELF. BY WASTING THE LIVES OF PIONEERING HEALTH PRACTITIONERS IN MYSTERIOUS WAYS. HEALTH PRACTITIONERS OFFERING PROVEN HEALTH REMEDIES AND SOLUTIONS WITH INFINITE DEDICATION TO THE WELL=BEING AND WHOLENESS OF ALL DESERVE RECOGNITION AND PEACE.

BARRY & NANCY

This couple soul portrait shows how both partners complement each other: It offered them a new understanding of each other, revealing their unique gifts, qualities, and tools for co creating everlasting passion, love and happiness. Opening portals to new perspectives, dimensions and realities brought them closer together. Being very "down to earth", a whole new world opened up for her, when she discovered a cherished departed loved one in the soul portrait. The two complement each other by their sensual, earthly and celestial realities and energies, a wonderful inspiration and support.

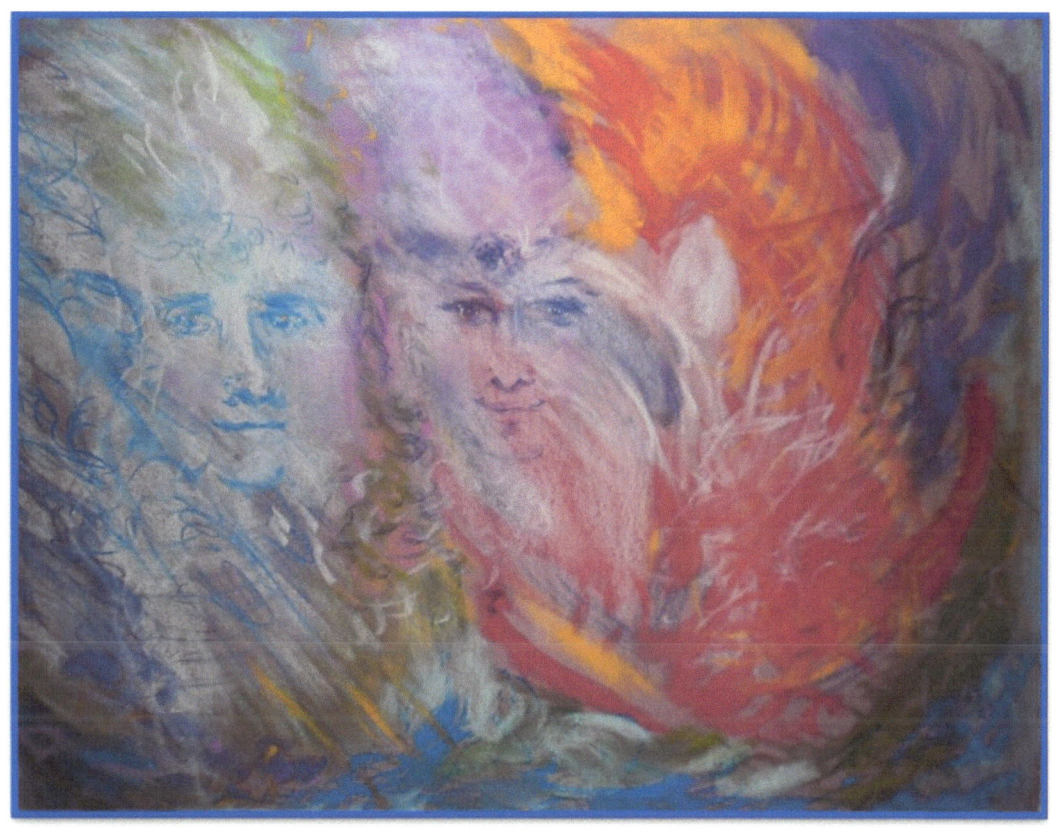

BARRY AND NANCY'S healing soul portrait required a four hour in-person session that included intuitive insights being shared with the couple regarding their relationship, other family members and more. In the months that followed this session, and with guidance from both the power of the portrait and Una's periodic telephone consultations regarding their relationship, Barry and Nancy announced their engagement to be married soon after the session. This couple's soul portrait shows how both partners complement each other.

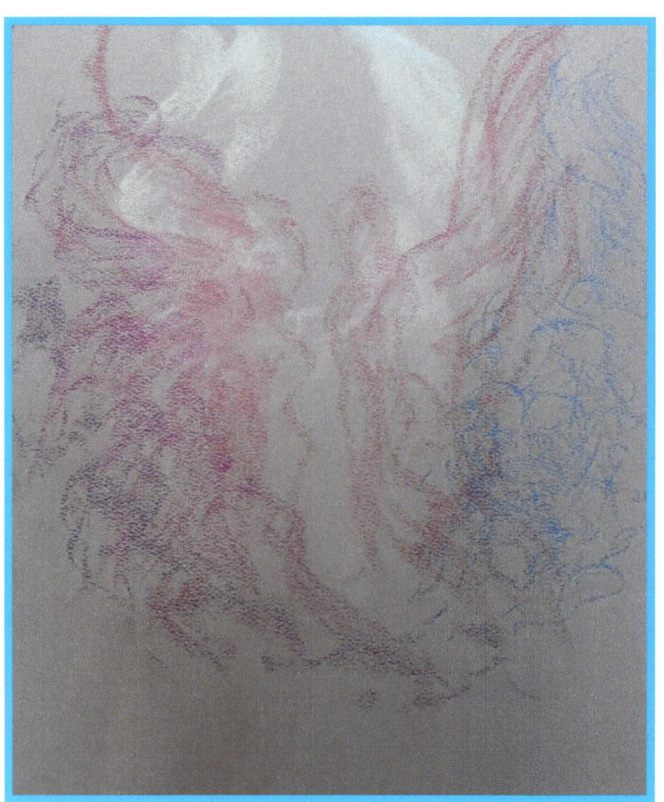
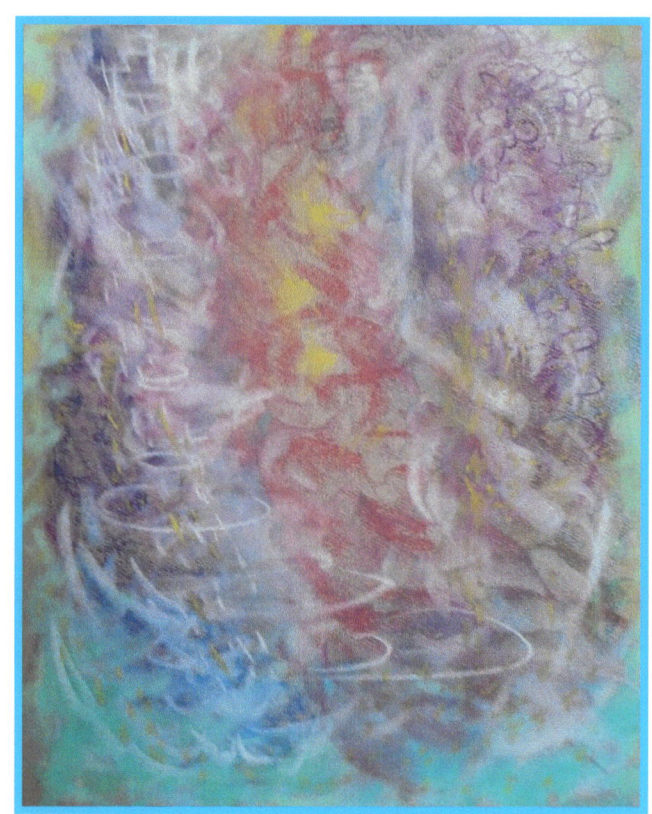

FALLING IN LOVE WITH MY DIVINE FEMININE INSPIRATION FOR CREATING A CENTER OF BLISS

Inspiring, I see myself in a palpable way..

EVOLUTION OF J. SOUL PORTRAIT
I embody and express the Divine Feminine that is Divine Love.
The two angelic beings of love in pink becoming one indicate the future potential union with your twin flame. Many angelic beings, ascended masters and Mother Mary are ready to assist you in realizing your soul's purpose and mission: The creation of a sanctuary inspiring personal and spiritual evolution, healing, wisdom,

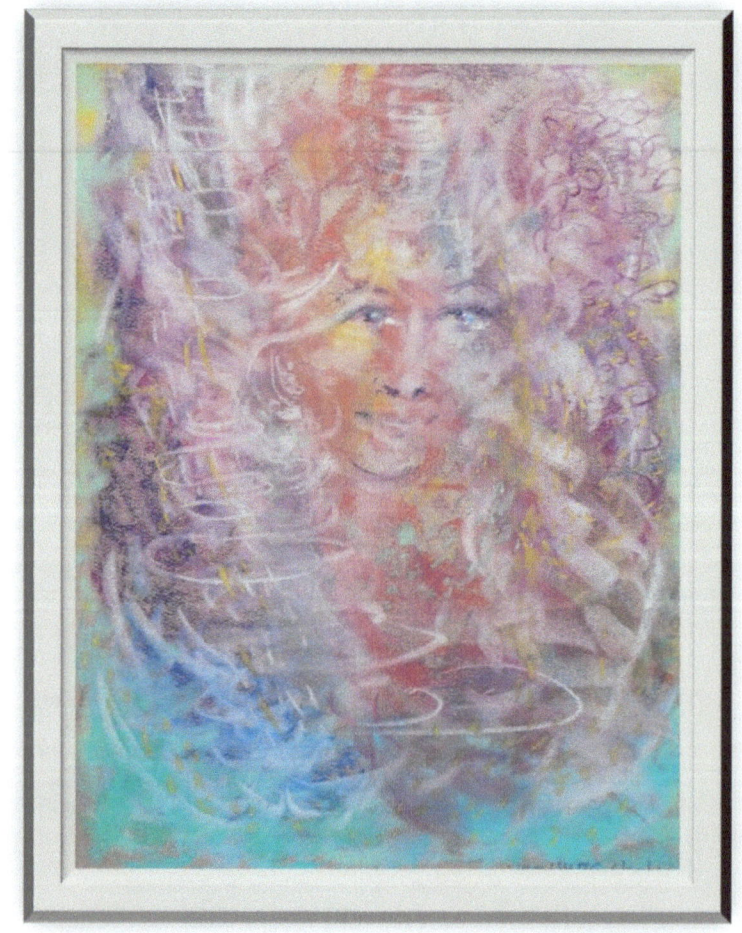

prayer, communion with angels, beings of light, and simply bliss. The tiger in the painting reminds you that you can achieve whatever you wish, with strength and determination. Helping people to see the blessings in their dramas, transforming sadness into joy, playfully with the dolphins present in the painting. White light coming down, a stream of Divine Light will support and inspire you at all times, Your magical tools (future side) will unfold. Let the power of your sweetness, grace, and unique Divine Feminine, simply LOVE, shine!

CHRISTINA FISHER

Soul portrait via photo. Christina resides in Maui, Hawaii, where she is a spiritual author, mentor and strategist; providing consulting for individuals and environmental and food safety, non-profits and seed projects. Christina is an exquisite author: From her book **Call to Unison – A calling inward to the Heart**: 'The Seven Tenets; where there is light there is Truth, where there is light there is Beauty, where there is light there is Wholeness, where there is light there is Love, where there is light there is Perfect Intention; Where there is light there is Unending Presence; Where there is light there is Sanctity of Purpose.

Christina was living on Kaui at the time I painted her soul portrait via photo. Totally transparent to cosmic vibration of light, Christina's soul portrait reveals her sacred journey into higher dimensions, universes, ancient times and past lives, opening new portals empowering her to channel ancient codes from the light through sacred writing and art. Kaui is a magical place that can facilitate access to higher dimensions of light, other universes, galaxies, past, present and future realities; if the person is in a state of peace, protected and attuned to their Divine Self. I am grateful for my soulful friendship with Christina. It is our goal and vision to raise human consciousness and to assist in co-creating a healthy planet earth.

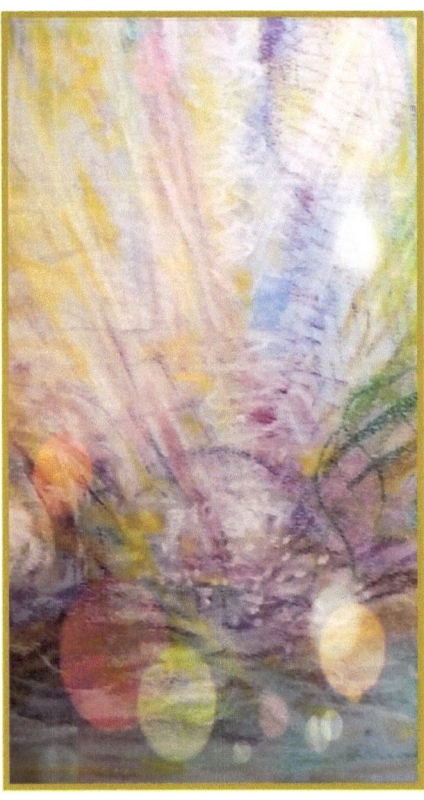 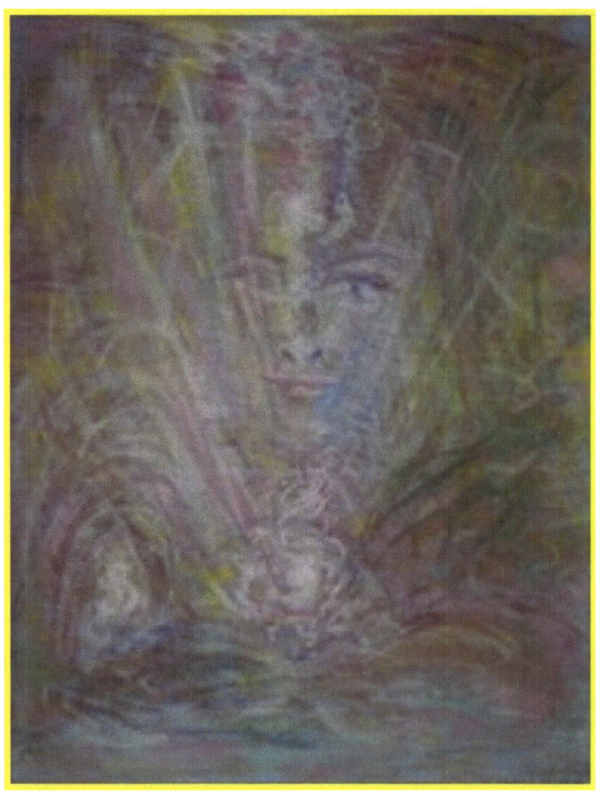

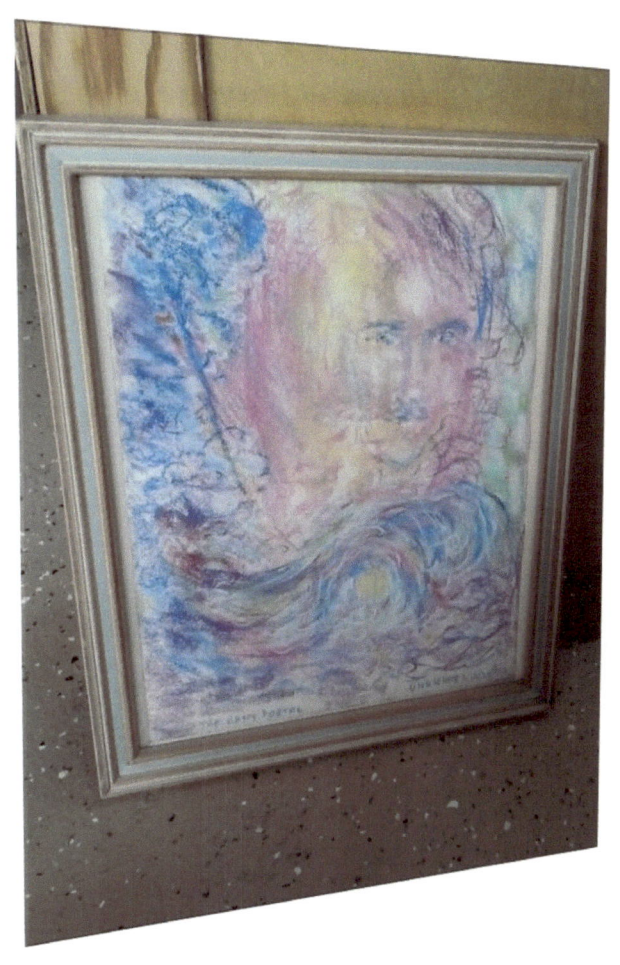

Scott "Sky" Masters

Compassionate communicator,
Creator of the 'Born to Bloom Center'

'THE HAPPY PORTAL'
created in San Diego

A portal to the inner Divine joy, that is innate within all of us and can never be destroyed. Accessing and enjoying the energy of inner joy and happiness, is a Well that is never-ending, always ready to flow into our body/heart and mind. Happiness is our birth right.

Scott's soul portrait reveals his incredible generosity, goodness, gentleness and wisdom. He truly is an earth angel. I am so grateful to have Scott as my dear friend.

Scott's testimonial:

Una's portrait called "Happy Portal" was a Divine gift during a time of grief for me. It washed away my sadness with vibrant colors in a spiral upward flow toward the positive aspects for my being and also healing of my inner child. I am so grateful to have this incredible visual and spiritual reminder of who I am and where I am going. Una's healing soul portrait has been a gateway and a portal to my greater Self, with all the guidance and inspiration from supportive beings on the Other Side, my teachers, angels, guides. I recommend Una's work that is a catalyst of inspiration and guidance for many years.

Brigitte

Wisdom, Declaration of love from a father to his beloved daughter(an executive for paramount pictures) via this soul portrait in pink. Prevented from connecting with her personally. This healing experience empowered him to pour the energies of all his love for her into her soul portrait revealing how he saw her: emanating nobility of body/mind/soul and spirit, radiating exquisite beauty, wisdom, infinite love and light.

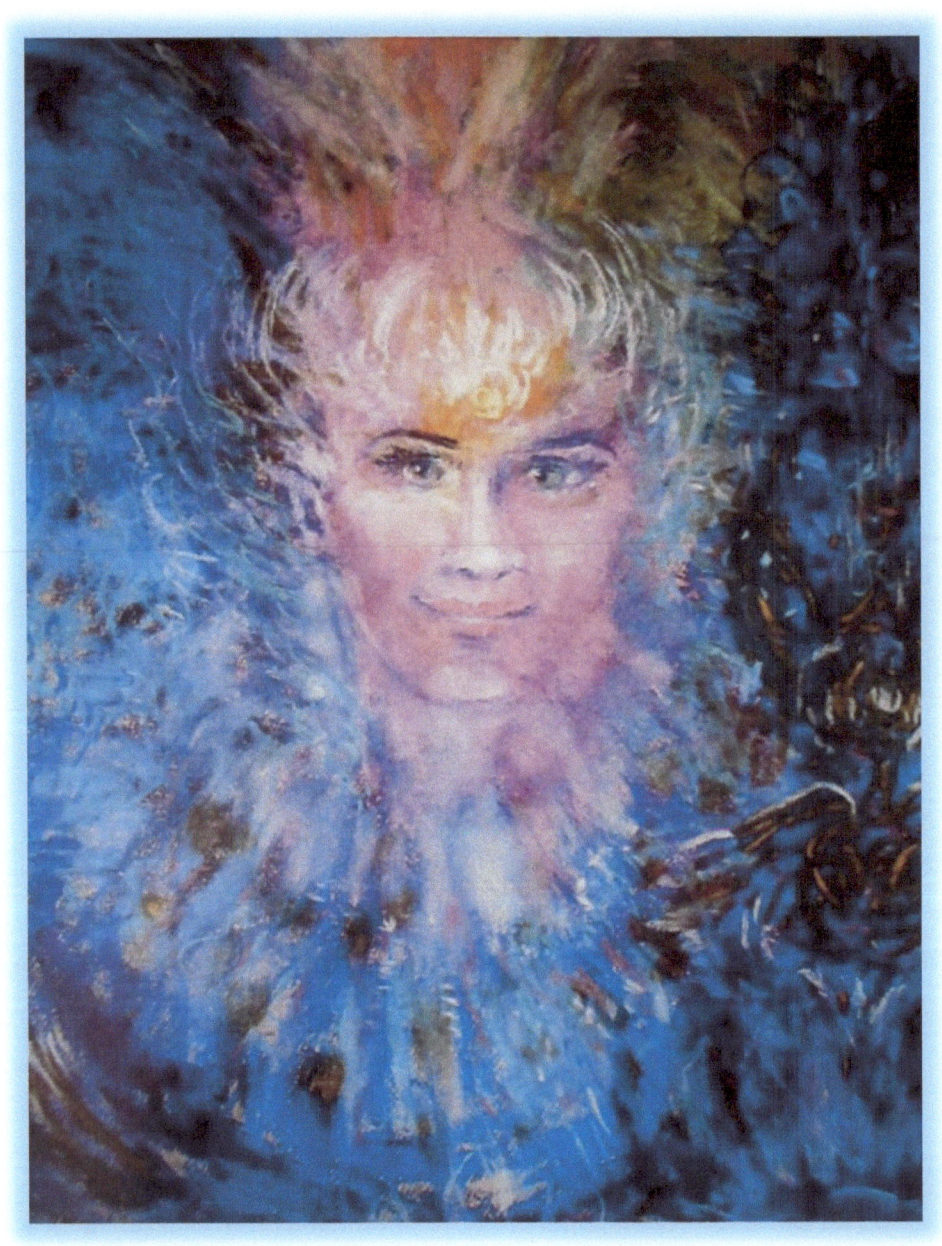

Darrell

Love is that which moulds into what we are meant to become. In Love we are all one. I experience myself in my soul portrait as the tender celestial poet, pure, timeless, crystal clear, transparent to inspiration and wisdom from celestial masters. Like a bird, I am free and boundless. I and the sky are endless with possibility.

Darrell, meditation teacher, poet, photographer - This soul portrait was a constant reminder of his intimate connectedness with the Divine Source and celestial guides giving him the strength, clarity and guidance to navigate through challenging times with serenity and faith in the Divine Love that never fails.

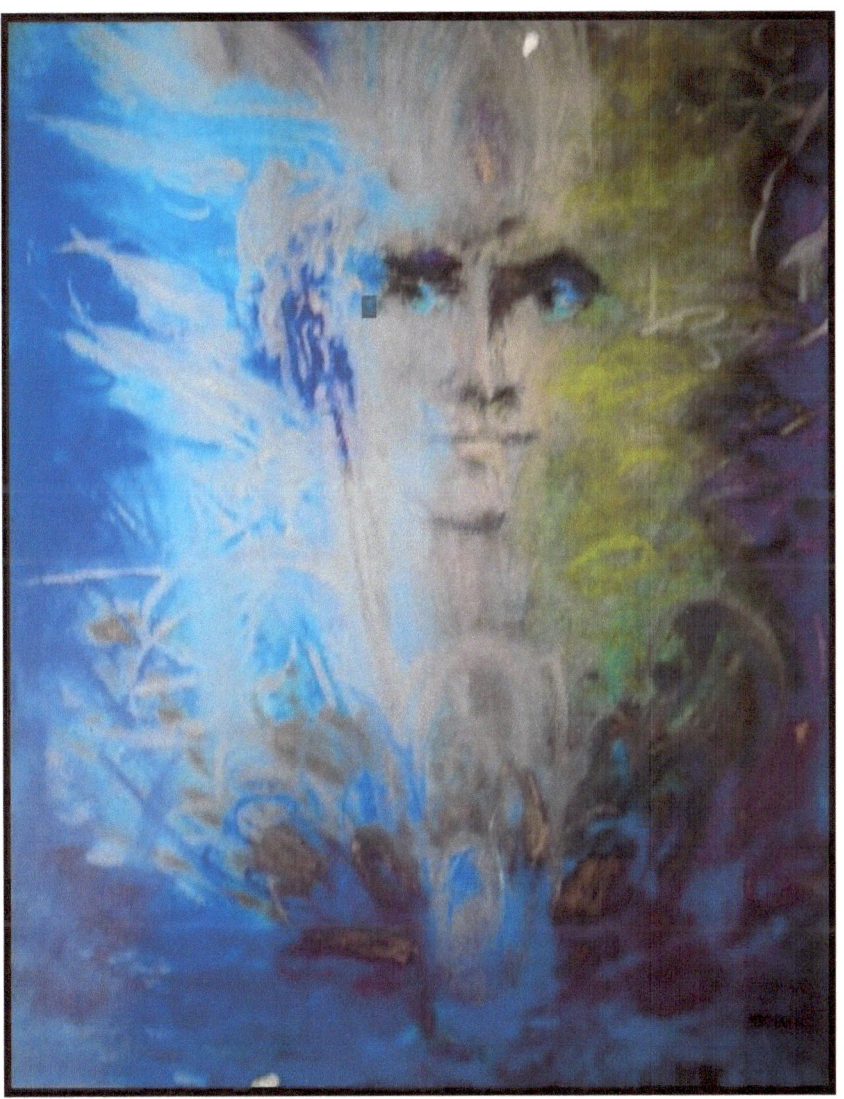

Cynthia Ochoa

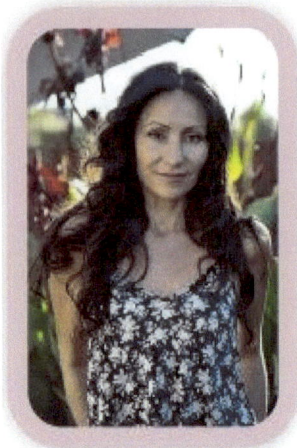

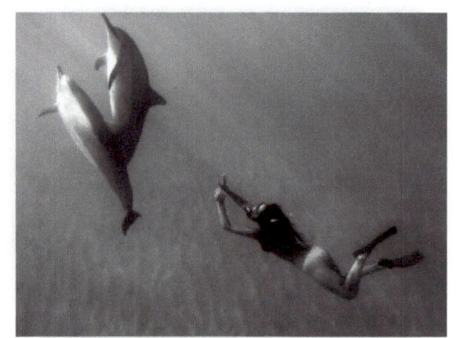

Transformational journey to new freedom expressing her gentleness, spiritual and creative powers, she finds her true vocation as a gifted video photographer of Dolphins; her beloved friends.

1. This purple soul portrait reveals her loving connection with St. Germain, the Ascended master, alchemist, with the gift of the purple flame. During the session St. Germain has become one with her, as her permanent guide, infusing her with purple light vibrations, offering gifts of support, inspiration and transformation for her new soul's journey.

St. GERMAIN, appearing always in purple, comes to us in many ways, assisting us to awaken our inner spiritual power, a new awareness of freedom, to release and transform relationships, situations etc. Accessing our inner, spiritual power connects us with our Divine essence, which helps us to illuminate the dynamics in our relationships from our soul's point of view, inspiring us to make the decisions aligned with our Divine Self, empowered by the love and wisdom of our soul. St. Germain helps to transform, transmute and clear whatever we are ready to release and heal. It is important to discover and connect with the guides especially assigned to us. They will lovingly protect, guide and inspire us on our path of life and love. The violet guidance was given to Cynthia bringing her to Hawaii where she has been blessed with communicating telepathically with these amazing beautiful creatures, the dolphins, as well as with the sea turtles and whales.

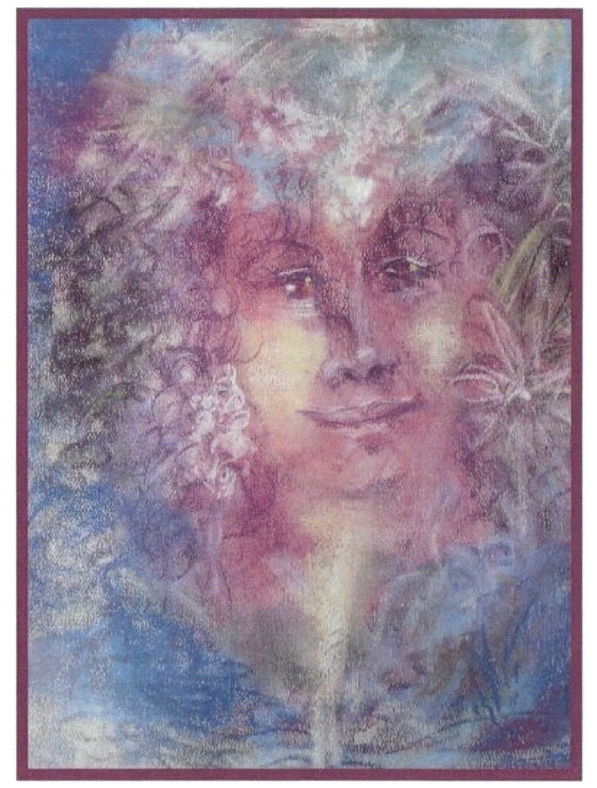

Mom Christina

SENDING A SMILE FROM HEAVEN, AMAZING GRACE, TENDERNESS, WISDOM AND BLISS; A COMFORT FOR THE SOUL AND SPIRIT OF HER DAUGHTER.

Excerpt of her testimonial: You truly captured her angelic Grace and Heavenly persona, delicate, elegant. I am ever so grateful to you for the way you were able to transcribe her visual portrait into words, as her message is pure and clear, The portrait is truly a fine reflection of all my mother's qualities. I can feel her sensitive quality and yet her strength also. She clearly exemplifies the Divine Mother. I feel her total presence and know she truly is likeness of the Feminine aspect of God. She has been by my side since her passing and she has assisted me so often. She has been a light and her eminence is truly lovely.

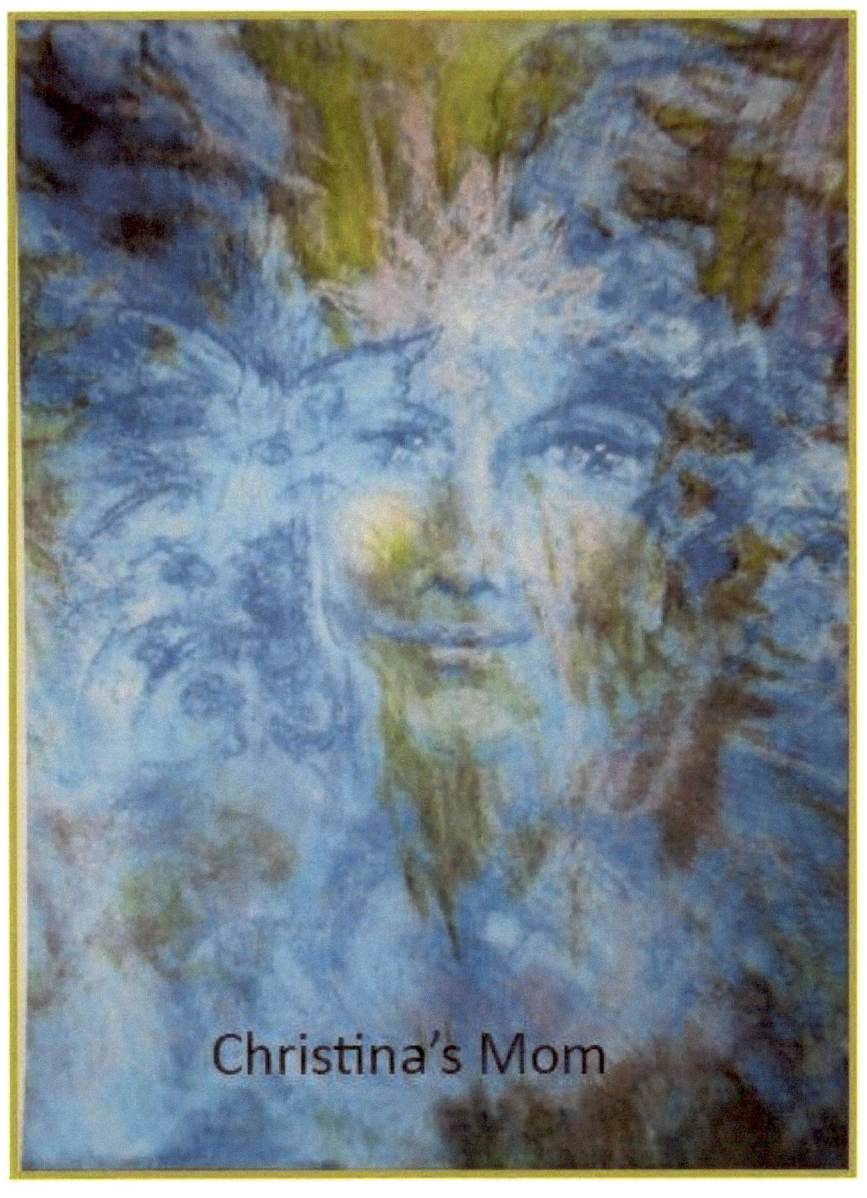

Christina's Mom

Healing Power of Aura & Soul Portraits

Kiana

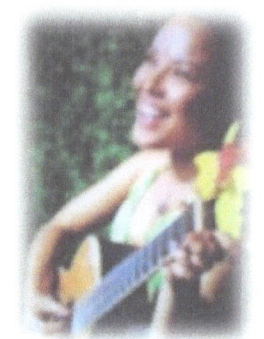

KIANA LUNA ~ Soul Portrait painted in Honolulu, Hawaii, in 2010. Kiana is an amazing internationally acclaimed singer/songwriter/musician, whose sacred music is dedicated to celebrating Love, Nature, Universal Truths, Self-Reflection, and the Oneness of God/Goddess within All Beings. In this painting~ Kiana's special angels of Love and Healing, along with Goddess Pele and her ancestors, are offering gifts of support, strength, guidance, clarity, and heavenly music, flowing through the stream of Love around her, into her, and to All she reaches~ expressing the Divine's reflection through her sonic vibrations. Kiana radiates nobility of body/mind/soul/spirit.

~KIANA LUNA'S ROLE AS A MUSICIAN IS TO PROMOTE THE BLOSSOMING OF HUMANITY~

"One individual who Lives and Vibrates to the Energy of Illumination, Bliss, and Infinite Peace, will Counterbalance the negativity of 10 million people who calibrate at the lower weakening levels." (Author Unknown) *~~Keep Shining and Sharing your Beautiful Spectrums of Divine Light, Dear Ones! Every little Spark & Rainbow makes a Difference~~*
  ^_^ *~~Kiana Luna ∞

QUOTE FROM KIANA: "We are United whenever we Choose the synchronization of Love over the

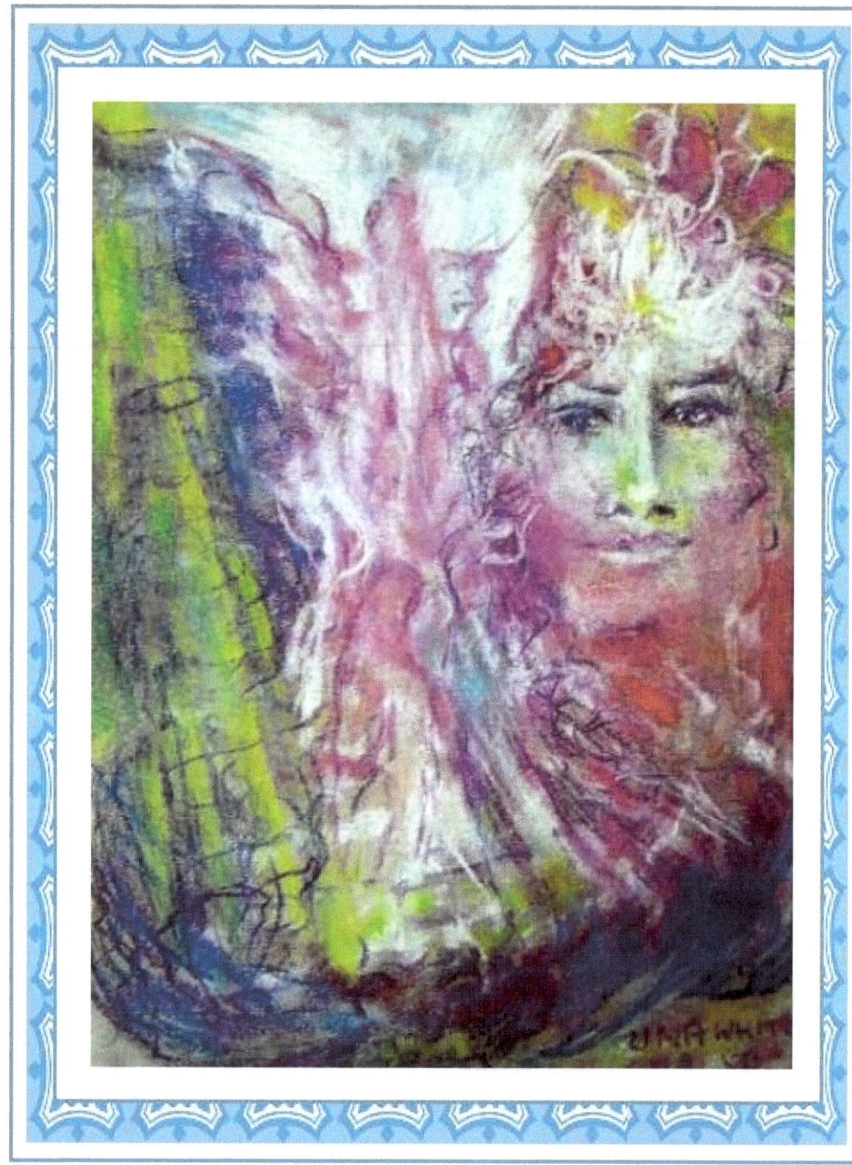

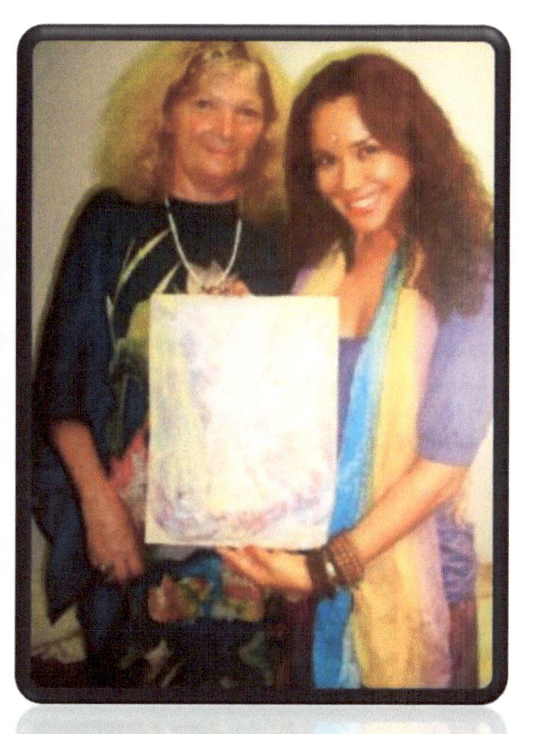

discordance of Fear and we can Peacefully rest in the Divine Knowing that~ whatever the Question~ Love is the always the Answer. May we All be Mindful of the Seeds we plant and Nurture, with every Energetic Contemplation, and may the rain falling in our souls during times of sadness~ Wash away the pain of our aching hearts~ And sprout blossoms of fragrant rainbows~ In every corner of our precious spirit's art."

http://www.KianaLuna.com
Facebook Music Page:
www.Facebook.com/KianaLunaMusic

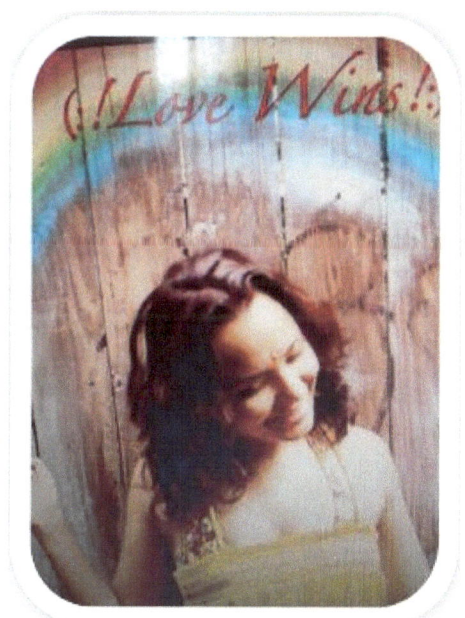
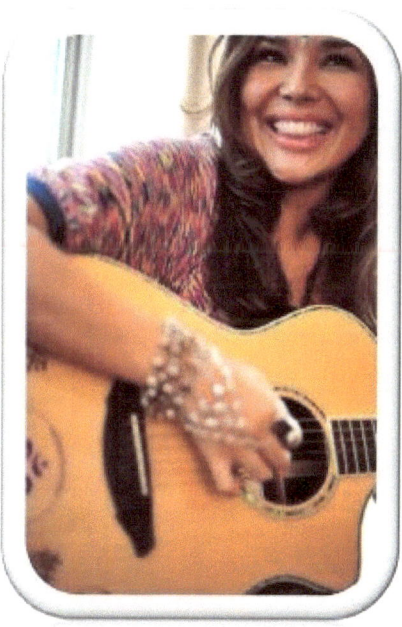
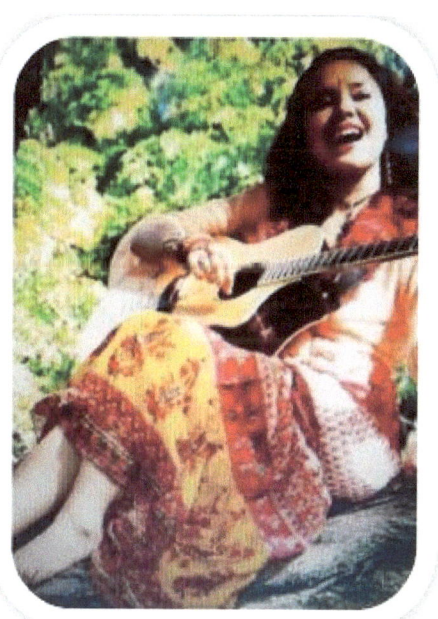

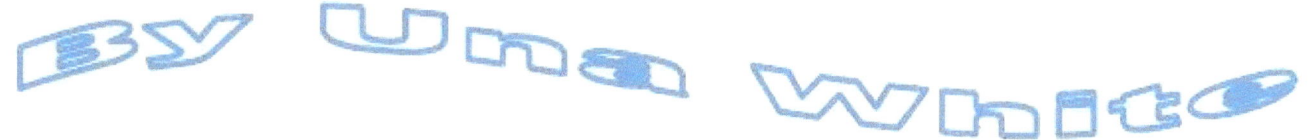

THIS SOUL PORTRAIT OF MICHAEL BAILEY is a reflection of his intimate relationship with nature, the animal kingdom and especially the dolphins.

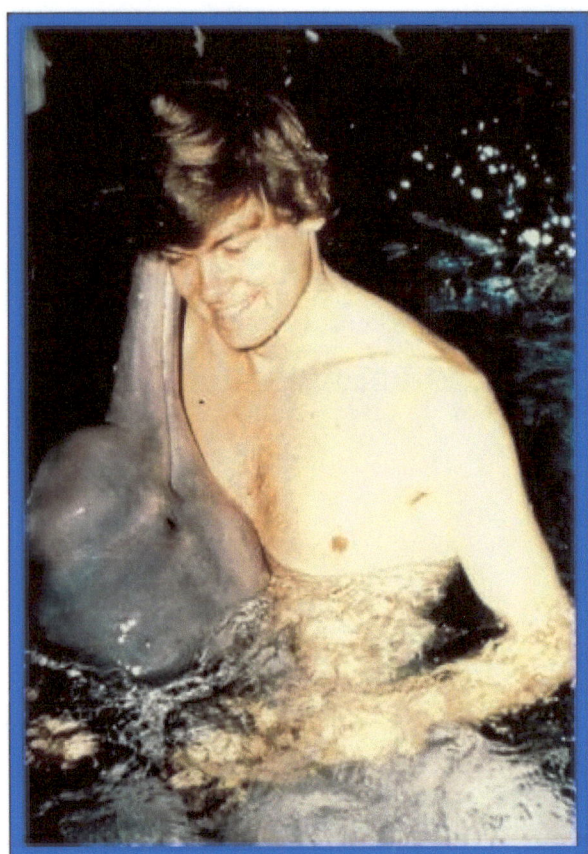

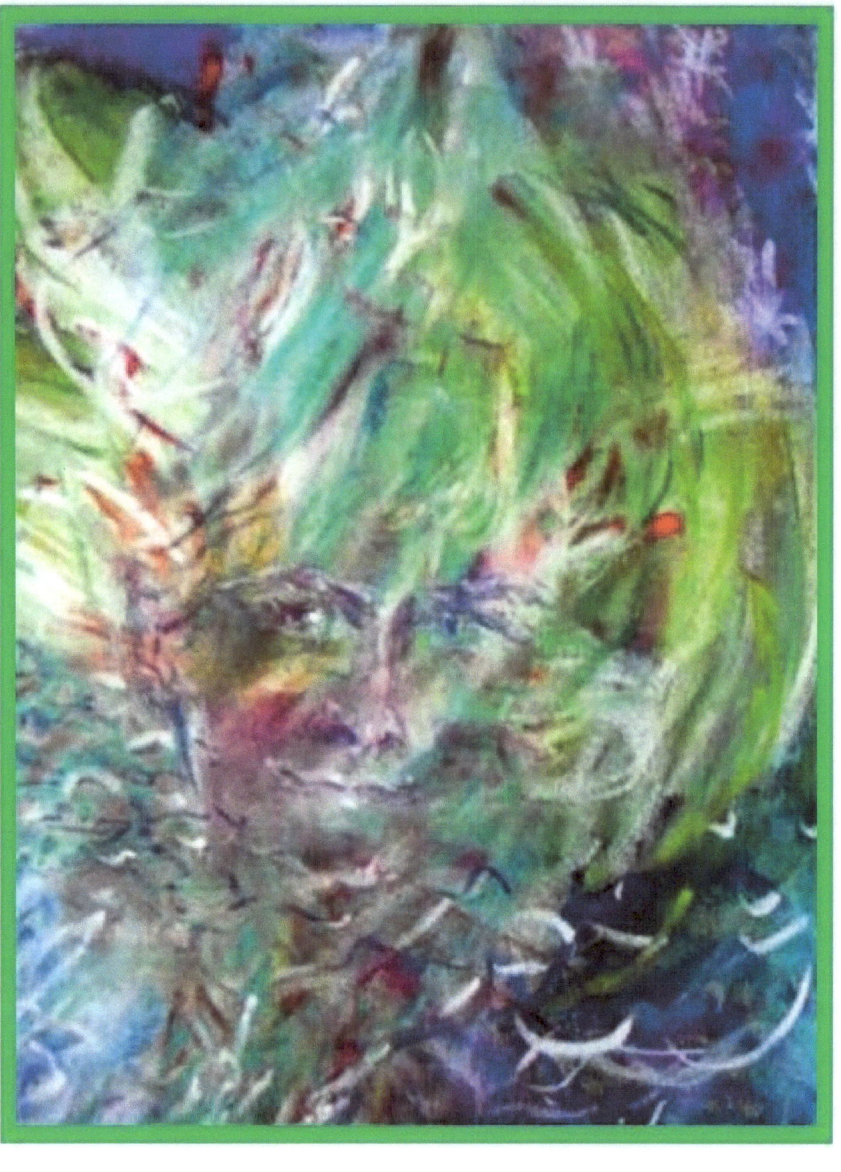

A visionary, Michael is very alert, focused, intuitive, courageous, persevering, adventurous, and with eyes like an eagle, Michael is a spokesman and activist for saving dolphins, whales and is dedicated to safe endangered animals in general, through his video graphic work, lectures; traveling worldwide. Dolphins, his guardians, are revealing to Michael portals to other dimensions to discover. Soon after this soul portrait, Michael was part of the famous movie THE COVE. www.planetviews.com. Making the World a Better Place for All. It takes immense effort, perseverance and courage to wake up the general public, to stop corporations from the unnecessary torture and killing of animals, just out of greed, pleasure and power. But we must not give up. In the end we, the humans will have to pay for our mistakes. May we all live together in peace respecting the animal kingdom and mother earth, so we can all blossom in harmony.

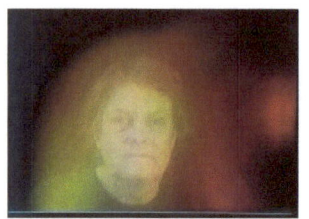

SOUL PORTRAIT OF AKAKA, GOVERNOR OF OAHU, SENATOR
painted in Honolulu in 2005: visionary, gentle, wise and compassionate, love of beauty.

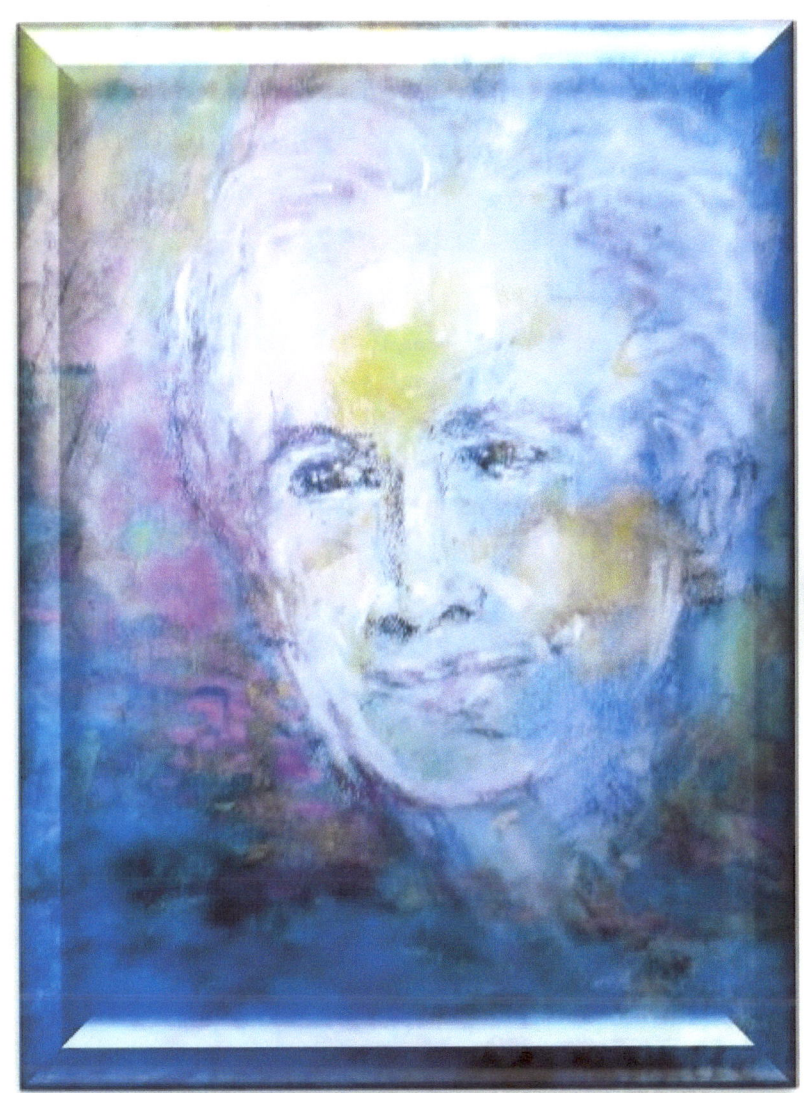
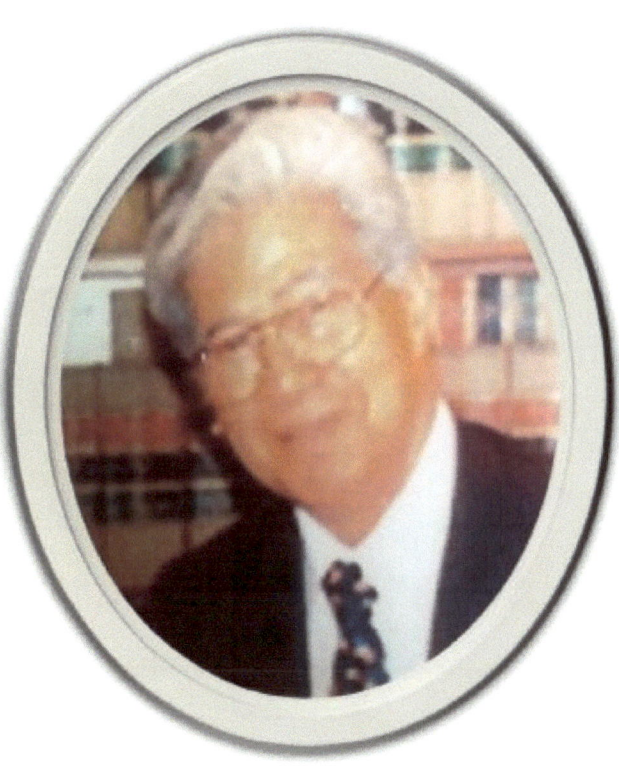

AKAKA, GOVERNOR OF OAHU AND SENATOR

After painting the soul portrait of his niece, she introduced me to him to paint his soul portrait, painted in Honolulu in 2005: visionary, gentle, wise and compassionate, love of beauty, devoted to the wellbeing of the people of Hawaii. He loved his soul portrait, it is in Honolulu in the government building and in Washington DC.

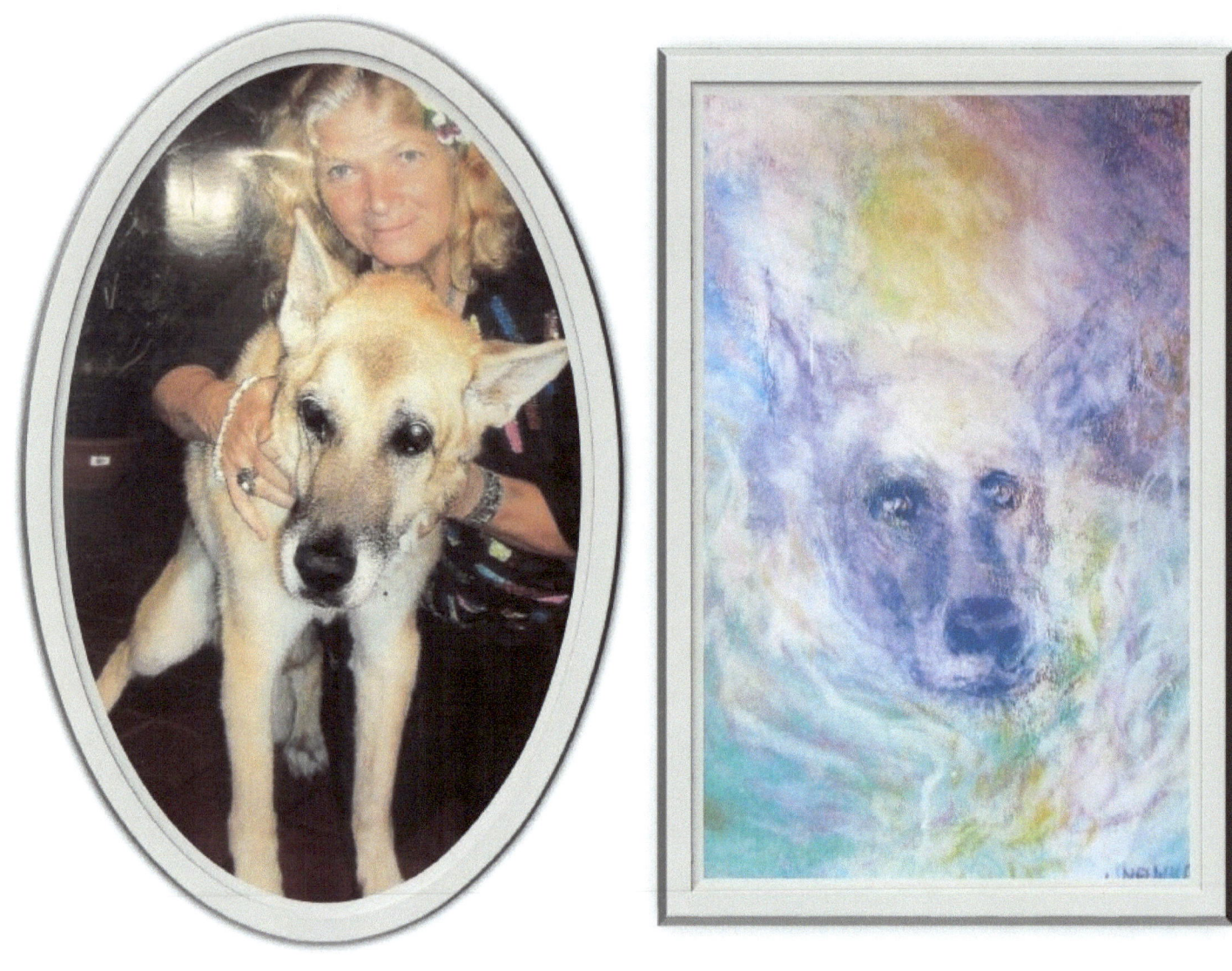

BARON, painted at the castle in 2008 in doggy heaven since 2010 Looking at you with mysterious eyes.

Baron, who's triumphant and healing spirit is living forever in our heart. Looking at us with mysterious eyes, he was touching your heart as he looked into your eyes. Loyal to his human soul friend Bruce, a mystic warrior, he waited for him to come home until his last breath. He and his guardian, Bruce, are part of the same soul family, comparing the two soul portraits.

There is never an accident why we choose a pet or why the pet chooses us. There is a sense of belonging and purpose which is different in every case.

Mutti Una (Mother of Una). Experienced as strict during the first part of my youth, my mother wants to be remembered as loving and beautiful. I am grateful to my mother, because I grew up in an artistic environment, because she was a curator of art museums in Vienna. Our love for art is deeply embedded in my DNA and has become my life love path. Mutti introduced me early in life to Leonardo da Vinci, who became one of my greatest heroes and inspirations for my art. Not agreeing with my wish to pursue art as a career because artists are poor, my Divine destiny made the decision for me: I was introduced to the director of the Academy of Fine Arts in Vienna, he was so touched by my art that he imposed my candidature onto his colleagues without any exam of admittance. My training as art therapist, the teachings and initiation to my Sufi name Una by Pir Vilayat Inayat Khan, have confirmed my commitment to be a spiritual artist/therapist/healer. Pir's teaching about the Divine light, and the importance to access and express our unique luminous Divine face, inspired me to translate the unique light and beauty of souls into luminous soul portraits, of people who desire to discover and see their beautiful Divine Self. I will always cherish my mother as my primordial inspiration of my art, her kindness, love of nature, devotion to us, and finally the discipline. "Thank you mutti" We only have one mother, it's important to be thankful and loving during her life time and forgive any weaknesses.

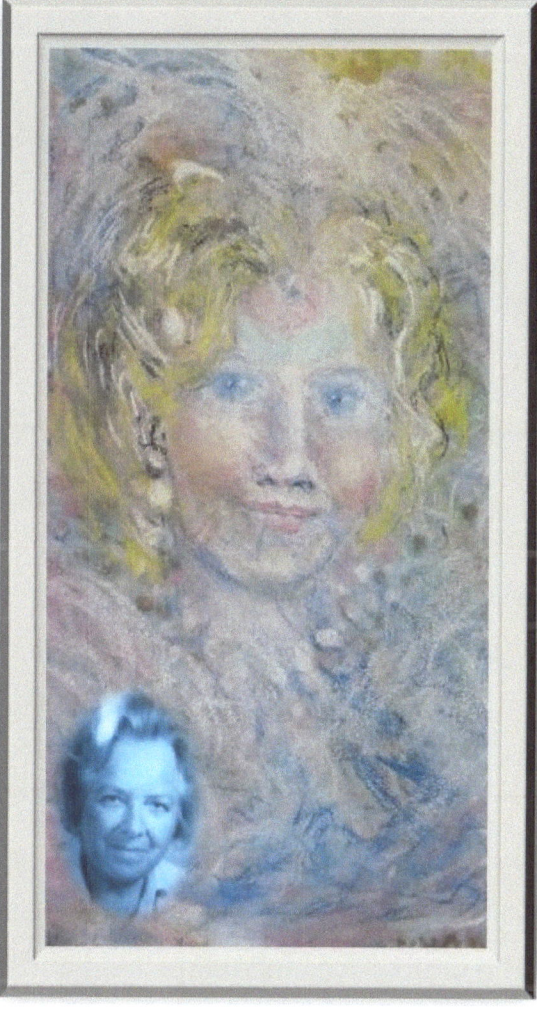

Sometimes we may understand our parents better when beyond the veil of love. It's never too late to reconcile. Love is mysterious, boundless, and life goes on.

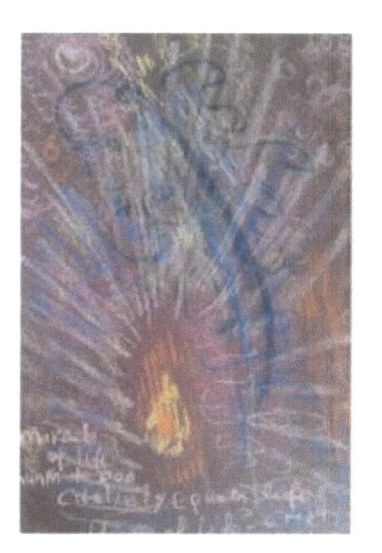

PORTAL OPENING TO HEAVEN. Painted at the same moment my mother passed, inspired by an intense flow of LOVE traveling from Vienna all the way to California on highways of love and light.

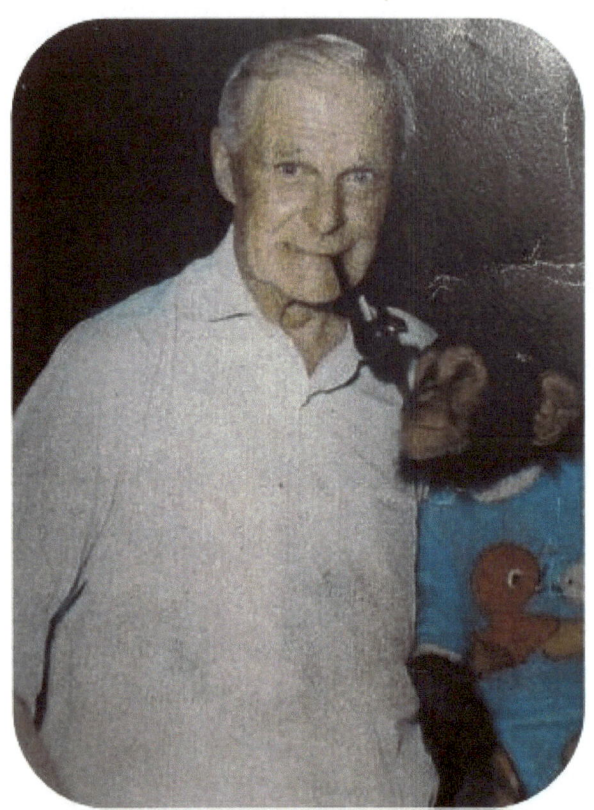

SOUL PORTRAIT DANCING INTO HEAVEN with his pipe:

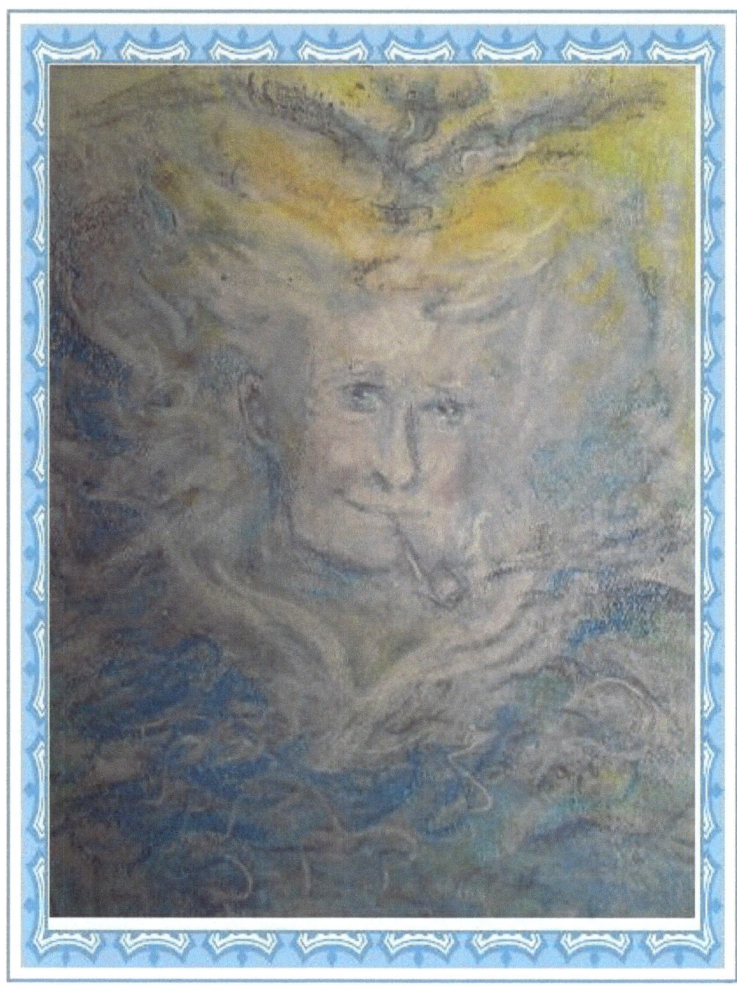

MY dad (Papi), transitioned on 9/9/1999 at 9 am at age of 99 years, it seems that this was his last joke. His life's journey was complete after a trip to Northern Germany by car (with friends) to see his old fatherland.

Expression of total peace, serenity, tranquillity, smiling. Peace has been his way of life; creating peace has, is, and always will be, important for me. Some of his qualities continue to live through me:

My father was good hearted, wise, a free spirit, optimist, a charming story teller, adventurer, traveler, loved the oceans, nature, animals, especially his pet, the chimpanzee. As the soul portrait faded after 16 years, I painted over the original, using a color photocopy of his original soul portrait. Guided as if by an invisible hand, his soul portrait transformed itself becoming younger and younger, he rejuvenated on the Other Side… still happily smoking his pipe.

PIR SAYS: I smile at you, do you feel my smile? Do you experience the smile of God? Just receive it, love it, and smile back.
And this Divine smile will be imprinted within your being. It will bring you joy, and the knowingness that all is well.

Streamed by Una White

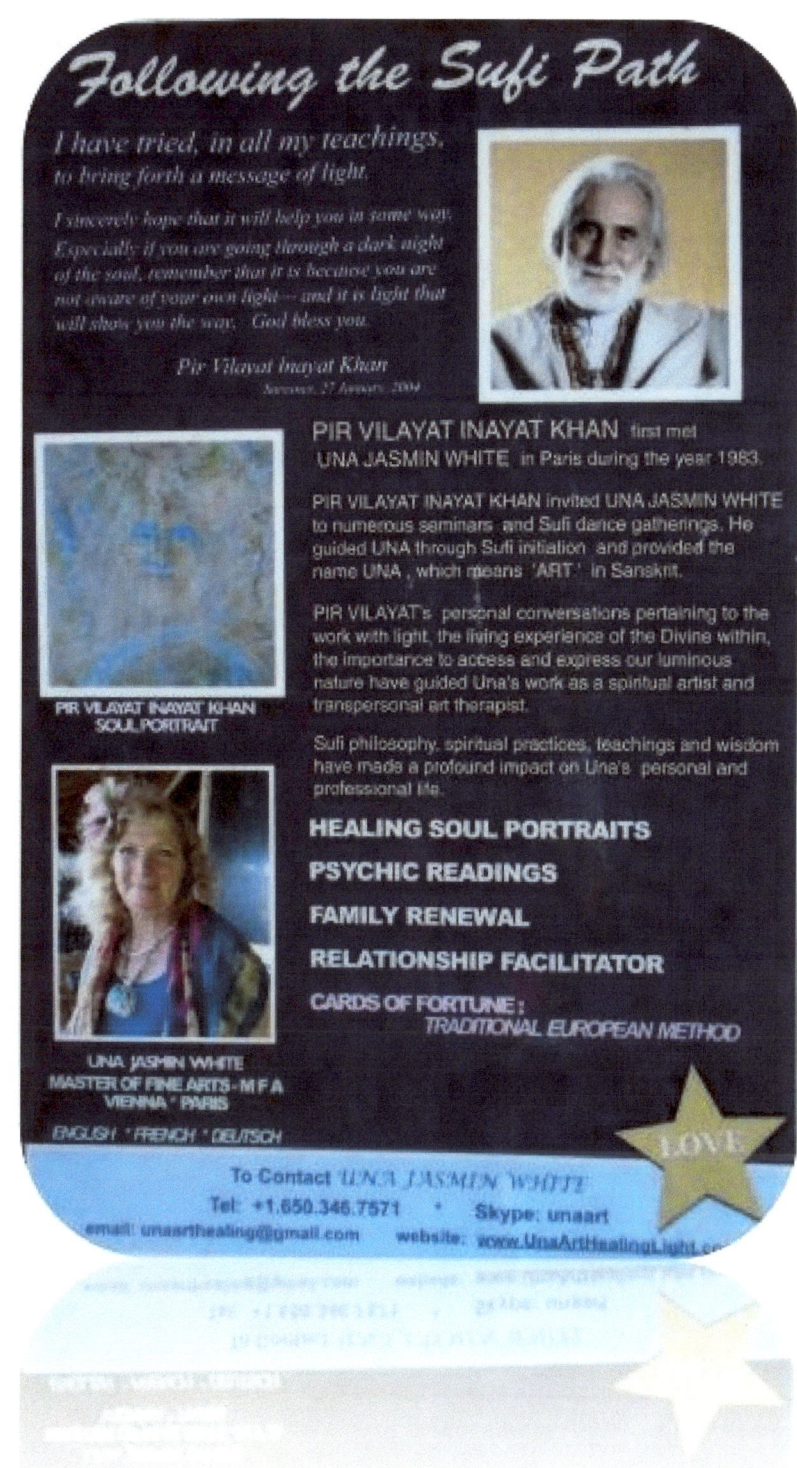

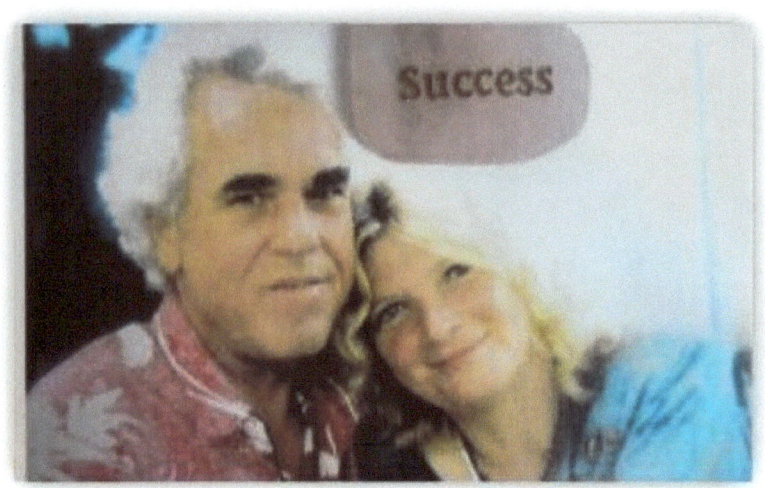 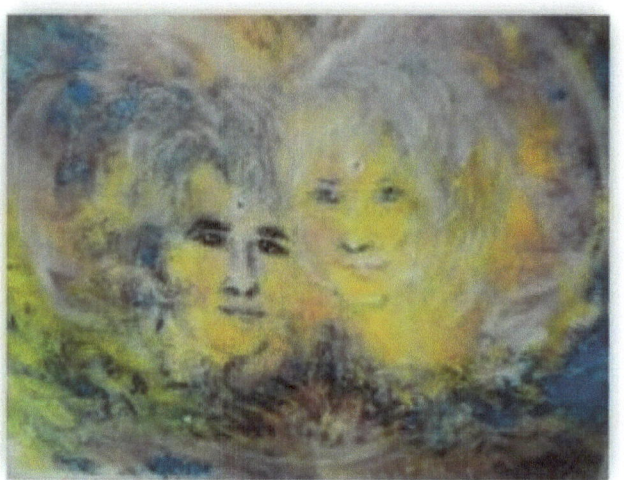

I am forever grateful for my sacred love relationship with John, who keeps inspiring me to co-create our work from the world of Light and to continue our legacy, knowing that **LIFE GOES ON, AND THAT LOVE IS BOUNDLESS. I AM COMMITTED TO UNITING HEAVEN AND EARTH** by painting celestial soul portraits of departed loved one, revealing the heavenly beauty and offering closure, hope, peace and guidance.

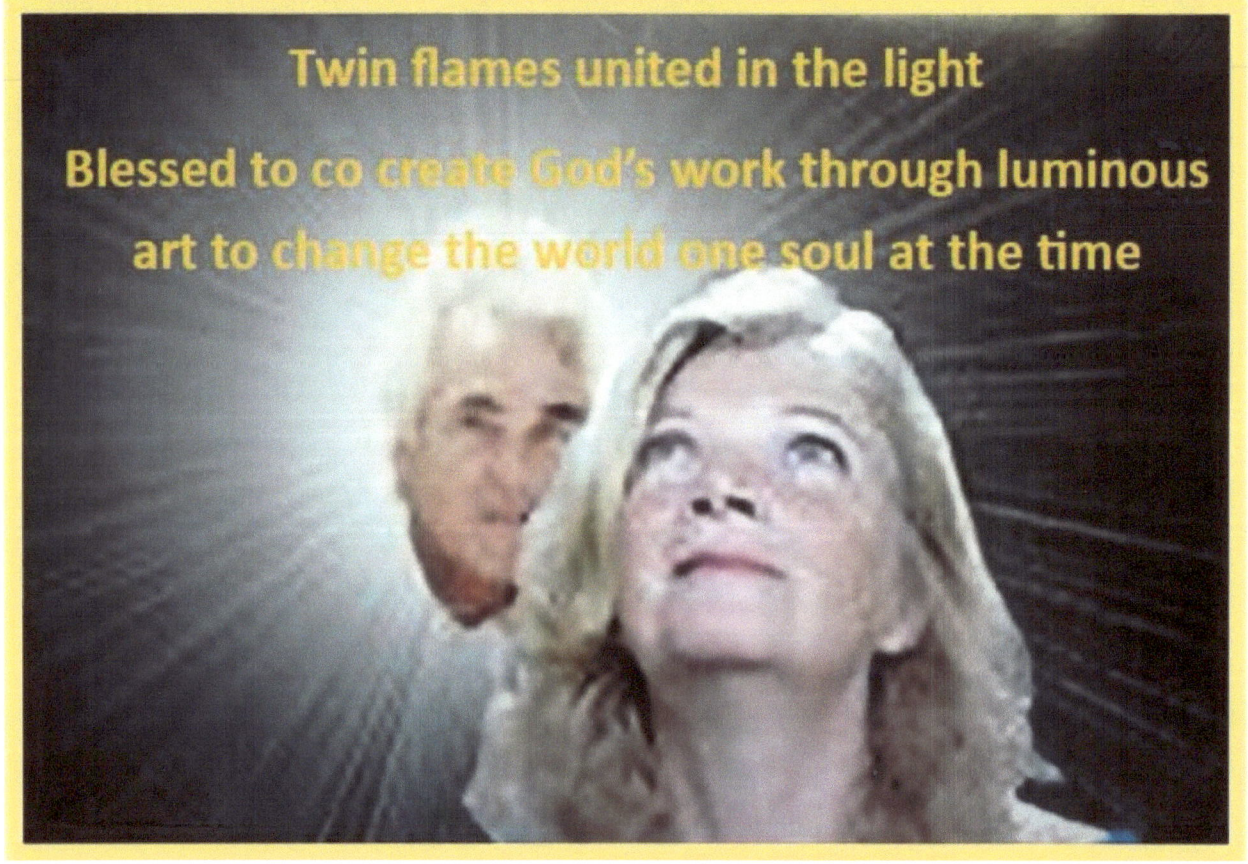

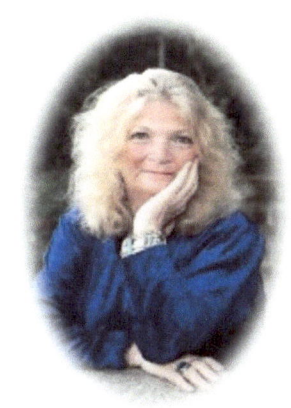
M.F.A. Academy of Fine Arts, Universities of Vienna and Paris. Cert. art-color Light Therapy. Psych Synthesis, England. Psychoanalysis, Paris. Cert. Reiki master teacher. Angel readings/healing, Doreen Virtue. Transpersonal art therapist, relationship healings. Una is an internationally acclaimed Soul Portrait Artist, Artistic Medium and Master Healer.

Una is truly blessed with the ability to connect the physical world with the non-physical realms and dimensions of light through her celestially guided healing art and her visionary healing soul portraits. Guided by her extraordinary artistic, intuitive and healing gifts, Una channels (streams) and captures the unique light and beauty of the soul, whilst bringing through life transforming messages and predictions from this and the Other Side. For over 30 years Una's pioneering healing methods have transformed the lives of thousands. Una has communicated her spiritual signature of Unconditional Love (as vessel of Divine Love, Wisdom, Light, and Beauty) through workshops, lectures, at universities, medical and holistic centers, Conscious Living expos, radio, TV shows, publications, CDs, mp3s in 3 languages, healing soul portraits, private counseling and healing sessions. Especially since the passing of her beloved husband it is Una's passion and commitment to 'unite heaven and earth' through her luminous soul portraits of cherished departed loved ones, revealing their heavenly beauty and wholeness, offering closure, loving gifts of comfort, hope, guidance, peace and healing; and the awareness that LIFE GOES ON, THE ENERGY OF LOVE IS ETERNAL, LOVE IS BOUNDLESS.

Testimonial by Christina Fisher, Maui, Hawaii, author & healer

"When you sit with Una White, you are transported into the world of light. You feel as though you are sitting in a radiant shower of Divine Love. Her portraits are illuminating your soul's truth, and capturing the essence of your Divine imprint. Una truly is a conduit for spiritual light and grace. And the information she provides is inspiring and truly accurate. She is a magnificent visionary anchoring high vibrational messages through her exquisite prism of color/light and sound."

ITS ALL ABOUT LOVE...

WHEN THE POWER OF LOVE OVERCOMES THE LOVE OF POWER, THERE WILL BE PEACE FOREVER

Love transmutes, transform, heals, unites
Love fills everything, every cell of our body/mind/soul

Love restores all that is to its natural state of Divine perfection. If we just listen to our heart, letting go of control, fear or any barriers,....

And gratefully accept the gift of grace with its many faces

By Una White, artistic medium/transpersonal art therapist, relationship mentor

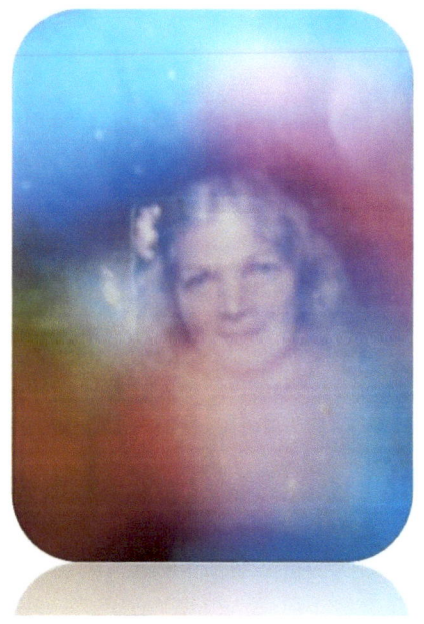

FB Una Jasmin White
YouTube Unawhitesoulportrait

www.ingramcontent.com/pod-product-compliance
Lightning Source LLC
Chambersburg PA
CBHW051203220526
45473CB00003B/880